Strapless

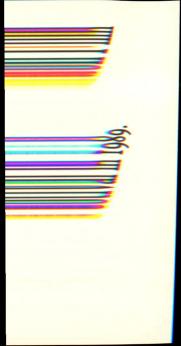

1989.

Strapless

DAVID HARE

faber and faber
LONDON · BOSTON

First published in 1989
by Faber and Faber Limited
3 Queen Square London WCIN 3AU

Photoset by Wilmaset Birkenhead Wirral
Printed in Great Britain by
Richard Clay Ltd Bungay Suffolk

© David Hare, 1989

A CIP record for this book is available from the British Library

ISBN 0–571–15498–0

For Rick

'She should never have looked at me.
If she meant I should not love her!'

Robert Browning
'Cristina'

Strapless was first shown at the London Film Festival in November 1989.
The cast was as follows:

LILLIAN HEMPEL	Blair Brown
RAYMOND FORBES	Bruno Ganz
COLIN	Hugh Laurie
GERRY	Billy Roche
MRS CLARK	Camille Coduri
MR CLARK	Gary O'Brien
AMY HEMPEL	Bridget Fonda
HUS	Spencer Leigh
MR COOPER	Alan Howard
ROMAINE SALMON	Suzanne Burden
HAROLD SABOLA	Cyril Nri
NURSE	Julie Foy
STAFF NURSE	Jacqui Gordon-Lawrence
CARLOS	Julian Bunster
MADELEINE	Gedren Heller
IMOGEN	Imogen Annesley
JULIA KOVAGO	Dana Gillespie
IMRE KOVAGO	Constantin Alexandrov
PRISONER	Stephen Holland
PRISONER'S BRIDE	Giselle Glasman
REGISTRAR	Edward Lyon
CROUPIER	Derek Webster
HELEN	Alexandra Pigg
JILL	Francesca Longrigg
NEIGHBOUR	Helen Lindsay
FAULKNER	Jeremy Gagan
PEVERILL	Clive Shilson
DOUGLAS BRODIE	Michael Gough
DAPHNE BRODIE	Ann Firbank
ANNIE RICE	Rohan McCullough
RICHARD FORBES	Joe Hare
PHIL	Liam De Staic
MARY HEMPEL	Kirsty Buckland
GIRL AT STATION	Melanie Roe

Director	David Hare
Photography	Andrew Dunn
Producer	Rick McCallum
Co-producer	Patsy Pollock
Music	Nick Bicat

PART ONE

OPENING CREDITS
*Under the credits, images of old Europe. The texture of crumbling
façades, stucco, sky-blue walls and pink plaster. Wooded hillsides,
dying blooms, mists in the mountains. Parapets and water.*

As the word STRAPLESS *appears, a stone statue of a woman,
holding up her dress with a single hand held over her breast.*

INT. IGREJA DA MADRE DEUS. DAY
*The face of the suffering Christ on the cross. He is made out of
plaster. His head is at an angle, looking down.*

Opposite him is LILLIAN HEMPEL. *She is American, in her
mid-thirties, with auburn hair, wearing a summer dress. Her
accent is East Coast, and her manner is assured. But she is
looking very slightly puzzled at Christ's expression. Then at his
side, where, in the place of blood from his wounds, they have put
fresh roses.*

In close up LILLIAN'*s hand as she reaches into her bag for a fresh
linen handkerchief. She drops it accidentally on the floor as she gets
it out. We watch as it flutters down on to the stone. Before she can
reach down, a hand takes it.*

*In long shot we now see the whole church. A man in a dark suit is
kneeling at* LILLIAN'*s feet, picking up the handkerchief, in front of
the altar. There are candles all round, and we now see the scale and
grandeur of a Renaissance church. The man is* RAYMOND FORBES.
He is a little older than LILLIAN, *with very dark hair, thick set. He
wears smart English clothes, and his manners are English, but his
accent is subtly foreign. There are little flashes of gold on his cuffs
and fingers. He has a slightly satirical air, as if very slightly amused
all the time by other people's behaviour.*
RAYMOND: You dropped this.
LILLIAN: Yes. Thank you.
      (*He stands a moment, as she takes it.*)
      I like the roses.
RAYMOND: They're the blood of Christ.
LILLIAN: Yes.
      (*Without having to move, he reaches across and lights a candle,*

I

which he sets among the others already lit around a small Madonna.)
Are you a Catholic?
RAYMOND: No. But I believe in being polite.
(He slips a large foreign note into the box beneath the statue. LILLIAN catches sight of this, then turns and begins to walk into the main body of the church. RAYMOND follows a couple of paces behind.
The faces of the devout in prayer. People are kneeling, muttering and throwing their eyes up to heaven. One man, particularly impassioned, is unconsciously speaking out loud to God.
LILLIAN frowns, thinking. RAYMOND watches.)

INT. IGREJA DA MADRE DEUS. DAY
LILLIAN and RAYMOND are now standing opposite a plate-glass window which is about twenty-five feet up in the air, giving on to the ornate golden church below. The effect of the height makes them seem to float in mid-air. We move in on their backs.
RAYMOND: Are you here for long?
LILLIAN: I'm sorry?
RAYMOND: In Europe?
LILLIAN: Just a week.
RAYMOND: Uh-huh. On holiday?
LILLIAN: Yes.
RAYMOND: On your own?
(She doesn't answer, but turns and strolls away from the window.)
I'm on my own. I'm heading south. I want to spend some time on the beach. Do you like the beach?
LILLIAN: My skin is too white.
(She frowns a moment, opposite a statue, brought up short.)
It's such a weird idea. I mean that Christ would take away your sins. That just by dying in some way he would make everyone's life better. *(Shrugs.)* I just don't get it.
RAYMOND: No. It's obscure.

EXT. PALAIS FRONTEIRA. DAY
They step out into the daylight, into the grounds of the church. A group of nuns is going up a flight of steps, leading some children to

2

the blue-tiled balcony which stretches away from us, covered in murals. It is hard to work out which part of Europe we are in.

LILLIAN: Well, thank you for the tour.

RAYMOND: Perhaps you'd like to have lunch.

LILLIAN: (*Quickly*) I've got a friend I must meet.

RAYMOND: Ah. I thought you were alone.

(*She looks at him a moment.*)

LILLIAN: I didn't say so.

RAYMOND: I'd swear you are.

(*There's a moment's pause.*)

LILLIAN: Well. I actually have to . . . see this friend of mine.

RAYMOND: You did meet me in a church. I mean, I must be trustworthy.

LILLIAN: Yes. I suppose.

(*She smiles. He waits.*)

All right. A quick lunch then.

RAYMOND: Excellent. I know somewhere.

(*He is about to move away.*)

Do you need to call your friend?

LILLIAN: Oh, later.
> (*She speaks very lightly. It's clear they both know no friend exists.*)
> Remind me. OK?

EXT. QUINTA DE SÃO SEBASTIO. DAY
A pistachio-green villa, with a white awning in front, which has been converted into a restaurant. Just five or six tables under the awning, with good linen and flowers between LILLIAN *and* RAYMOND. RAYMOND *is smiling at her from across the table.*
LILLIAN: Why are you laughing?
RAYMOND: I'm sorry?
LILLIAN: You're smiling all the time. As if something were funny.
RAYMOND: Oh.
LILLIAN: Perhaps I'm being stupid. But I don't quite get the joke.
> (RAYMOND *looks, as if weighing up whether to go into it.*)
RAYMOND: No, you're right, it's rude of me. Sorry.
LILLIAN: Is there something?
> (*The* PATRONNE *appears beside* RAYMOND. *An older woman, distinguished, tanned.*)
RAYMOND: See what this lady wants.
LILLIAN: The fish.
RAYMOND: Pizza for me.

EXT. QUINTA DE SÃO SEBASTIO. DAY
Later. LILLIAN *has pushed aside a piece of fish.* RAYMOND *has a pizza napolitana.*
LILLIAN: No, in fact I've just reached the end of quite a long relationship.
RAYMOND: Was it unhappy?
LILLIAN: Unhappy? Why, no. It was fine. What makes you say that?
> (RAYMOND *is looking at her as if he knew everything.*)
> I mean, it's none of your business.
> (*He is looking at her absolutely straight, matter of fact. She thinks a moment.*)
> He was an actor.

4

RAYMOND: Uh-huh.

LILLIAN: He's a good actor. He's also a very nice man.

RAYMOND: But?

LILLIAN: But nothing. Things got a little bit stale between us. Perhaps it's my fault. I do love the early part. I love the early days when love is given freely.

(*She suddenly stops, conscious that she seems to be flirting, which is not at all what she intends.*)

Now I'm embarrassed.

(*He is looking at her steadily. She tries to divert, picking up her fork to tackle her fish again.*)

RAYMOND: I like love freely. I like it freely as well.

EXT. QUINTA DE SÃO SEBASTIO. DAY

Later. They have puddings.

RAYMOND: I like the open air. I miss it if I'm too long away.

LILLIAN: Oh, do you?

(*There's a slight pause.*)

I like horses.

RAYMOND: Uh-huh.

(*A moment, as if they've now run out of things to say. She looks down at his hand, which is resting on the table, one finger tapping slightly.*)

LILLIAN: Where do you live?

RAYMOND: Lately? I've been spending time in Canada. I have a wonderful houseboat on a lake. Forty minutes out of Toronto, and yet you're absolutely alone.

LILLIAN: Is Toronto your home?

(*He shrugs.*)

RAYMOND: Toronto . . . London . . . Tokyo . . .

(*He smiles. From his pocket he takes out a small computerized clock. On its face is the name of every major city in the world.*)

You name the city. It tells you the time.

(*He punches 'LONDON'. In close up we see '2.30' come up on the digital display.*)

LILLIAN: Shall we get the bill?

RAYMOND: There's no bill. They know me here.

(LILLIAN *frowns, confused.*)

EXT. QUINTA DE SÃO SEBASTIAO. DAY
Later. LILLIAN *pushes her coffee aside, and makes to leave.*
RAYMOND: Will you come back to my hotel?
LILLIAN: No. (*Suddenly outraged*) No, absolutely not.
RAYMOND: Why not?
    (*She pauses a moment, a little taken aback by his directness. She is slightly flustered.*)
LILLIAN: Well, for a start, it's lunchtime. It's far too early.
RAYMOND: Will you come later?
LILLIAN: That's not the point.
RAYMOND: What is the point?
LILLIAN: I'm not coming.
    (RAYMOND *is looking across at her. It's hard to tell if she's actually amused. Certainly there is a reasonableness in the exchange.*)
RAYMOND: I don't want to be rude, but, er, you don't sound very convinced.
LILLIAN: Well, I am. I mean, really.
RAYMOND: It's clear. It's quite clear what's best for us to do.
    (LILLIAN *just looks at him.*)
LILLIAN: I shall spend the afternoon in the cathedral. With my guidebook. And you can spend the afternoon on your own.

EXT. QUINTA DE SÃO SEBASTIO. DAY
They move away from the house, towards the garden. Then stop.
LILLIAN: Thank you.
RAYMOND: Not at all. I enjoyed our relationship. Why not meet me tonight? We could do it again.
    (*He hands across a small card.* LILLIAN *looks at it.*)
    This is my hotel. Seven thirty?
LILLIAN: I don't know. We'll see.
    (*He smiles.*)
RAYMOND: Fine. I'll see you then.
    (*He opens the door to the street.*)

INT. HOTEL. EVENING
A smart hotel room. Decorated in perfect taste. A modern bathroom.
RAYMOND *has just showered. He is in perfectly creased dark trousers and a perfectly laundered shirt. He walks into the bedroom, picks up a tie from the dressing table, at the same time scooping up a*

6

*gold Rolex and gold cufflinks. There is a sustained excitement in the
perfection both of his clothes and his actions. He stands a moment,
perfectly dressed, and looks round the bedroom.*

EXT. STREET. EVENING
LILLIAN, *strolling thoughtfully alone along a Lisbon street. People
are promenading, window-shopping. The lights from the shops are
beginning to glow at just the moment dusk turns to night.* LILLIAN
*seems content, dreamy, but her slow rhythm contrasts in the cross-
cutting with Raymond's higher activity rate.*

INT. HOTEL. EVENING
RAYMOND, *coming tripping down the main staircase of this grand
hotel. He greets all the bellboys and porters, all of whom seem to
know him. He asks the* HALL PORTER *to order him a car. He
heads confidently towards the gilt and glass front entrance of the
hotel.*

EXT. STREET. EVENING
LILLIAN *looks across a small square to the grand entrance of the
hotel. The* HALL PORTER *is already there, looking for a car. She
stops on the far side, unseen, as* RAYMOND *comes out, the very
model of a successful businessman.*

We look a moment at LILLIAN. *Then she turns and walks
thoughtfully away, back in the direction from which she came.*

Her back as she vanishes down the busy street.

Fade to black.

PART TWO

INT. HOSPITAL CORRIDOR. DAY

LILLIAN *comes out of a ward into the corridor of a large general hospital in central London. She is wearing a white coat. Round the corner is the main lobby of the hospital, a scene of rampant chaos, full of waiting patients, some out-patients, some in pyjamas, trolleys, nurses, housemen, bleepers going, phones ringing, receptionists running – an NHS hospital stretched to the very limit, more like a railway station on a bank holiday.* LILLIAN *moves through it, hailed at once by* COLIN, *a junior radiographer, who is tall, thin, nervous, in his late twenties, also in a white coat. He has a messy shock of hair and there are food stains on his school-like tie and Viyella shirt. She does not pause.*

LILLIAN: Hello, Colin.

COLIN: How are things?

LILLIAN: Fine.

COLIN: How was your break? Was it wonderful?

LILLIAN: I think I saw every church in Europe. (*To a* PATIENT) Good morning, Mr James.

COLIN: Have you seen Cooper?
  (*She shakes her head.* GERRY, *an Irish doctor, approaches with a pile of files, which he puts, one by one, into her arms.*)
GERRY: That's yours.
LILLIAN: That's very kind of you.
GERRY: That.
LILLIAN: Good.
GERRY: And that. That too. And that.
LILLIAN: Well, thank you.
  (*She starts thumbing through the files as she moves along.*)
COLIN: There's meant to be some big departmental shake-up.
LILLIAN: Shake-up or shake-out?
  (*Before he can answer, a black* SISTER, *formidable, has taken* LILLIAN *by the upper arm and is pulling her firmly out of frame.*)
COLIN: I don't know.
SISTER: Dr Hempel. This way.

INT. CONSULTING ROOM. DAY
LILLIAN *is sitting in her white coat across a desk from* MRS CLARK. *The room is functional, with pale, institutional colours. The window overlooks the River Thames. There is a bookcase of medical books and a glass door which looks on to the hospital corridor.* MRS CLARK *is about twenty-seven, in a miniskirt and bright modern coat. She is small, peroxide blonde and Cockney.*
LILLIAN: What will you do?
  (MRS CLARK *does not answer. She is overwhelmed, on the verge of tears, unable to speak.* LILLIAN *waits a moment, tender.*)
  Your husband has an inoperable area of cancer. He has a spinal tumour. If radiation doesn't ease it, we have palliative drugs.
MRS CLARK: He's only thirty.
LILLIAN: I know.
  (*She looks down at the desk, waiting for* MRS CLARK. *She is very tactful.*)
  With our help he can get better for a while. We're not offering a cure. It certainly means he will suffer much less.

We can prolong his life. Perhaps for a year or two.
(MRS CLARK *looks up. Tears are pouring down her face.*)
I know. It's very hard.

INT. HOSPITAL WARD. DAY
MR CLARK *is sitting up in bed. He does not look ill. An Irish labourer, he has the face of a young Brendan Behan. He smiles easily as* LILLIAN *arrives,* MRS CLARK *a few paces behind.*
LILLIAN: There you are, Mr Clark.
MR CLARK: Good morning, doctor.
LILLIAN: How are you?
MR CLARK: I'm fine.
  (LILLIAN *smiles at* MRS CLARK.)
LILLIAN: I've now spoken to your wife. Why don't you talk
    things over with her? As you know, we would like you to
    stay in, initially at least, for a course of radiotherapy.
MR CLARK: I don't want it.
LILLIAN: I understand that. But it will help you fight any
    possible paralysis.
MR CLARK: I've just got this tingling in my feet. It's nothing.
    (LILLIAN *waits a moment, saying nothing.* MRS CLARK *moves
    towards the bed.*)
MRS CLARK: Thank you. Let me talk to him now.

INT. LILLIAN'S FLAT. EVENING
LILLIAN *pushes open the door of her flat by leaning against it. It's dark inside. It's off the Finchley Road, in North London, where the rooms are bigger than you find in other parts of London, cream-painted, with original mouldings. It has been furnished in a very wild, romantic, nineteenth-century style. The hall is dominated by an enormous, dark, Scottish landscape painting in the style of John Martin. A kilted Highlander standing on a mountain against an enormous glowering sky. There are chandeliers and antiques along the length of the central corridor, many of them covered with books and papers. It all has a sort of rotting, seedy grandeur that is completely individual.*

  LILLIAN *stoops down and picks up her mail. We follow her as she pushes open the sitting-room door and turns on the light. Whatever style was once in this room has been destroyed and made*

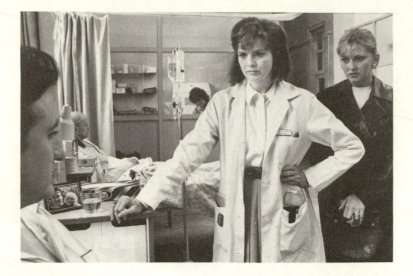

chaotic by a sofa-bed which has been set up right in the middle of it.
AMY *wakes the moment* LILLIAN *comes in. She's curled up on the
bed in a T-shirt and leather trousers. The sheets and pillows are very
messy. She's also American, dark-haired, in her mid-twenties, small
and thin, like a grown-up child; wild, anarchic, natural.*

LILLIAN: Hi. How are you?
> (*She does not stop for a second, as she continues on her way to
> open the curtains, letting in the afternoon light. At her feet, she
> sees a young man, curled up asleep. He has a couple of cameras
> round his neck and other photographic junk on the floor near
> him.*)
> Who's this?

AMY: He's called Hus.
> (LILLIAN *barely pauses to look down critically at his
> fashionably unshaven face asleep on the floor.*)

LILLIAN: Hmmm. Well, I wouldn't.

AMY: I didn't.
> (LILLIAN *goes through the door at the far end of the sitting
> room.*)

LILLIAN: Well, good for you.

INT. LILLIAN'S KITCHEN. EVENING
LILLIAN *sets down her mail and her bag on the counter in the small,*

white-painted kitchen and, still in her coat, puts on a pan of water.
AMY *appears, sleepy, beside her.*
AMY: Are you going out?
>(LILLIAN *shakes her head.*)
> To the theatre?
>(LILLIAN *is getting a packet of frozen food from the fridge.*
> AMY *automatically turns on a CD-player which blasts out rock*
> *music at an unbelievable volume.* LILLIAN, *without pause or*
> *thought, turns it off, just as automatically, as she returns to the*
> *counter.*)

LILLIAN: I'm not going to the theatre. I'm never going to the
theatre again. Ugh! Actors!
>(*She has taken out a boil-in-the-bag sachet and now puts it in*
> *the heating water.*)

AMY: Come out with us. It's going to be funny.
>(LILLIAN *has started going through her mail, horrified.*)

LILLIAN: Is this the phone bill? Jesus, how long are you
staying?
>(*But now* AMY *puts a photo in front of her of Prince Charles,*
> *in polo trousers, stripped to the waist.*)
> My God, where did you get that?
>(AMY *has picked up Lillian's mail as she puts it down, her eye*
> *caught by an expensive blue envelope with an elaborate red rose*
> *in the corner, hand drawn.*)

AMY: I like the look of that one.
>(LILLIAN *sees it for the first time. Takes it from her.*)

LILLIAN: Do you? I don't.

EXT. STREET. NIGHT
Click click click goes HUS, *photographing the inside of a restaurant*
from outside. He is ducking and weaving about in a manner which,
from the outside, looks vaguely ridiculous.

  Across the street, parked under a lamp-post, is an old American
charger car. AMY *and* LILLIAN *are sitting on it,* LILLIAN *in a*
damp mac. It is raining. Behind them, desolate urban landscape.
LILLIAN: Is this it? Is this what we're doing?
>(AMY *gives her a look, as if she's not worth answering.*)
> Do you do this all night?
>(*Across the street,* HUS's *behaviour is becoming more and more*

extravagant, on one knee, bending to one side, up against the glass.)

AMY: Don't you like his jeans?

LILLIAN: I'm sorry?

AMY: I was just thinking what great jeans he had.

(*Suddenly, as a couple comes out of the restaurant, HUS barges to the open door and begins photographing a group of diners. Suddenly one of them, seeing him, gets up in panic, his hand in front of his face. He's a half-known prince.*)

EXT. STREET. NIGHT

Later. HUS *comes across the street to join them.*

AMY: What did you get?

HUS: Enough. Minor royalty.

LILLIAN: Really? Which one?

HUS: Which one?

LILLIAN: Yes.

(HUS *looks completely blank as he gets into the car.*)

HUS: Which one? I mean, they're all princes. Don't ask me which one is which.

INT. HUS'S FLAT. NIGHT

A developing tray. Darkness but for the red bulb. The photo is coming through. AMY *is looking over* HUS's *shoulder. The prince with his arm round a girl.*

AMY: So, have you got it?

HUS: Got it.

(HUS *takes it out of the tray and turns the light on. He and* AMY *come out into the main area of what seems to be an abandoned central London warehouse, which he has done almost nothing to convert. Wire mesh has been left in place, to divide areas up. There is no sign of domesticity: just a mattress on the floor, beside a paraffin stove. Otherwise, discarded cartons and boxes of photographic equipment. The windows have all been boarded up.* LILLIAN *is sitting on a high shelf, from which her legs dangle. She has an air of amused tolerance.* HUS *holds the picture up.* HUS *smiles at* LILLIAN.)

I guess I've got about three hundred quid.

LILLIAN: Is that what it's worth?

HUS: The great days are over.

13

AMY: Except for Diana. Especially in a swimsuit.

HUS: Yeah, that's still twenty thousand.

AMY: Bikini: fifty thousand.

> (AMY *bites into a pizza.*)
> Best of all, bikini and pregnant.

HUS: Bikini and pregnant? Unbelievable.

AMY: Bikini and pregnant, you need never work for the rest of
your life.

> (LILLIAN *examines the wall of photos of Di, Charles and
> Fergie, some of which have been obscenely defaced.* HUS *is
> putting the photos in an envelope.*)

HUS: I have to take this for the first edition. Help yourself to
anything you want.

LILLIAN: Jesus, look at this!

> (*She has just noticed one photo pinned up among all the others.
> It is the only one not of royalty.* AMY *is shown, with no clothes
> on, being embraced by a naked black man with huge muscles.*
> LILLIAN *is shocked, but when she turns she sees that* HUS *has
> not noticed, and is standing by the door speaking very quietly to*
> AMY.)

HUS: Will you be here later?

AMY: (*Shakes her head.*) No, I'll be gone.

> (HUS *goes, trying to look cool, but truly sad. He says nothing*

more, but goes out, giving LILLIAN *a moment to hide her shock at the photo to which she now points.*)

LILLIAN: What's this? Your new passport photo? Don't send it
    to Ma.

AMY: Oh, yeah, she called me. She wants me to go back. She
    says she's lost one daughter already. I don't know. I'm
    having fun here. I meet a lot of funny people.

    (LILLIAN *looks at* AMY, *so at home on the awful sofa in the bare room with the unpacked crates for furniture, the remains of old takeaway meals.* AMY *sits, incomparably at ease, while* LILLIAN *thinks. Then* AMY *looks at Lillian's bag which is open on the sofa. The same blue letter is peeking out of the bag, still unopened.*)

You haven't opened your letter.

LILLIAN: I know. For some reason I'm scared.

INT. HOSPITAL WARD. DAY

LILLIAN *and* GERRY *together approach* MR CLARK's *bed. He is laughing and joking with three nurses as* LILLIAN *arrives.*

LILLIAN: How are you, Mr Clark?

MR CLARK: I'm feeling terrific.

LILLIAN: Well, that's good. I'm glad we persuaded you to stay.

MR CLARK: I like the life. It beats working on a building site.

(*The nurses all giggle.*)

I think it's worse for the wife, don't you, really?

LILLIAN: Yes.

(*She doesn't. She just smiles.*)

INT. MR COOPER'S ROOM. DAY

MR COOPER *is sitting behind his desk in his consulting room. Around him are ranged the team of doctors and radiographers who work with him in the department – about twenty in all in various stages of seniority. The chairs have been set out in a semi-circle, specially brought into the small room.* MR COOPER *is in his late fifties, bald, Scottish, judicious. Among those in the department are* HAROLD SABOLA, *and* ROMAINE SALMON, *an earnest junior radiotherapist in her late twenties.* LILLIAN *is sitting next to* COLIN.

MR COOPER: We have to face a period of almost infinite contraction. This won't come as news to anyone here. No one has been hit harder than this particular hospital. In the last six months we've closed two general wards. All we're doing now is holding the line.

(ROMAINE, *in the front row, frowns.*)

ROMAINE: With respect, Dr Cooper, I think we all feel these facts are familiar. I think what we're asking is, what you're going to do?

MR COOPER: Do?

SABOLA: Are you going to allow job cuts?

MR COOPER: It's not at my wish. People will find themselves
not reappointed. Nobody's job is safe any more.

(ROMAINE *looks round for support.*)

ROMAINE: You see, the reason a lot of the younger doctors
wanted this meeting was because we feel it's time to stick
our necks out and make a formal protest to the
government.

(MR COOPER *looks down.*)

MR COOPER: It's not for me to say. Everyone must make up
their own mind.

INT. HOSPITAL CORRIDOR. DAY

The whole team shambling down the corridor. In the front group,
LILLIAN, SABOLA *and* COLIN, *who is eating a Mars bar. He looks*
meaningfully back at ROMAINE *who is five paces behind.*

GERRY: Well, that was pretty startling. Is that him at boiling
point?

LILLIAN: Oh, yeah. He's beautiful when he's angry.

(*They smile.* COLIN *throws a panicked look back at* ROMAINE
who is in an animated conversation with a nurse.)

COLIN: Watch out. She's bound to ask you.

LILLIAN: Who?

COLIN: Romaine. Well, someone's got to do it.

LILLIAN: Do what?

COLIN: Lead the protest. Be the figurehead. It's obvious.
You're the universal auntie.

LILLIAN: Oh, really?

(SABOLA *shakes his head.*)

SABOLA: I don't understand. Why doesn't everyone just burn
down Downing Street?

LILLIAN: I don't speak the language, remember? I've only lived
here twelve years.

(*She heads off.*)

EXT. STREET. NIGHT

A side street in Swiss Cottage. There's not much traffic about. It's
tree-lined. A STABLE BOY *is leading a large chestnut-brown horse*

17

down the street. It walks contentedly along, clip-clopping on the
pavement.

INT. LILLIAN'S BEDROOM. NIGHT
The bedroom is pretty and ordered, neat compared with the living
room where AMY *is camping out. There are Chinese screens, paper*
lamps giving a warm pink light on to the bed where LILLIAN *is*
lying, reading a book. She is wearing a silk Chinese dressing gown
over jeans and a T-shirt. The sound of rock music in the rooms
beyond. She looks up as AMY *comes in.*
AMY: Do you have a bra?
LILLIAN: Yes, sure.
> (*She nods at a drawer in a cupboard, meanwhile getting up*
> *from the bed.*)
> There's a drawerful.
AMY: Are we making too much noise?
LILLIAN: No, I can't sleep anyway . . .
> (*She wanders past* AMY *who is still sorting through the drawer,*
> *and walks aimlessly down towards the sitting room.*)

INT. LILLIAN'S SITTING ROOM. NIGHT
LILLIAN *comes through to find the sitting room transformed into a*
photographic studio. There are eight or nine people in the room and a
riot of umbrellas, lights and cameras pointing at an improvised dais,
which is backed by an enormous piece of photographic paper. AMY
comes into the room behind her.
AMY: Lillian, this is Carlos. He's Argentinian.
LILLIAN: Hello.
> (CARLOS *smiles back. He's swarthy, dark-haired, twenty-five,*
> *charming. He replies in Spanish. On the dais a tall, red-headed*
> *girl of twenty-three called* MADELEINE *is pinning pieces of*
> *material in eccentric patterns on to a living model,* IMOGEN.)
AMY: Madeleine's teaching me designing.
LILLIAN: Well, good. I'm sure that's very useful.
AMY: Yeah, you know. Dresses.
LILLIAN: (*To* MADELEINE) I thought you were a model.
MADELEINE: I was.

LILLIAN: Like Amy's a secretary.

MADELEINE: You're only a model until you can be something else.

(*She smiles across at* AMY, *who is giving the model the bra. A black girl is sitting on the floor talking non-stop into the phone.* HUS *is playing with the motor on his camera. Two girls are smoking dope in the corner, side by side, identical joints, identical Walkmans.* CARLOS *has gone to the window to close the blind, but now he sees something in the street that distracts him.*)

CARLOS: Hay un caballo fuera en la calle. Hey, Amy.

(AMY *frowns and goes over to the window. She looks over* CARLOS's *shoulder. We see their point of view. On the opposite side of the street are some railed gardens, and by them the horse is standing, waiting under the lamp-post. The* STABLE BOY *is standing near by.*)

AMY: How extraordinary. It's a horse. Look, Lillian.

(LILLIAN *is standing alone at the sink, making coffee. She has the coffee-grinder in her hand, but her actions are now halted. At the word 'horse' she is completely still. The others have all gone to the window.*)

LILLIAN: What?

AMY: Why don't you come here?

EXT. FLATS. NIGHT

The Victorian entrance to the block of flats. LILLIAN *has put on a pullover but she still wears her Chinese robe on top as she quickly comes out into the street. She walks across the street. She's angry.*

LILLIAN: What the hell's going on?

(*The* STABLE BOY *looks a little surprised, but from behind the tree next to him* RAYMOND *appears. He is in a suit.*)

RAYMOND: You said you like horses.

LILLIAN: I knew it was you.

RAYMOND: Of course it's me. Didn't you get my letter? It said exactly when I was coming.

(*He looks puzzled.*)

Well?

(*She stands, angry, not able to speak.* RAYMOND *waits a moment, gestures, then speaks very quietly.*)

Look. I bought you a horse.

(*She stands, biting her lip. She's lost. She walks a few paces away.*)

(*Quietly*) I found a stable. Don't worry. I'll pay for it. You can ride every day in Hyde Park.

(*There's a silence. A car goes by. The horse takes no notice.*)

LILLIAN: How did you find where I live?

RAYMOND: I rang all the hotels in the town where I met you. One gave me your address.

LILLIAN: Well, they shouldn't. It's fucking well illegal.

RAYMOND: I wouldn't have done it if I'd realized that.

(*He is looking at her steadily, presumably sending her up. But it's hard to tell. She avoids his eye.*)

LILLIAN: What's his name?

RAYMOND: Heartfree.

LILLIAN: He's very beautiful.

RAYMOND: Yes.

(LILLIAN *is looking at the horse, who is very calm.*
RAYMOND *speaks in the quiet tone of a seducer.*)

He's just two years old.

(LILLIAN *turns back to him, mistrustfully.*)

LILLIAN: I didn't open your letter.

RAYMOND: Why not?

LILLIAN: Because I knew it would get me into trouble.

RAYMOND: Trouble? What kind?

(LILLIAN *takes a quick look at the* STABLE BOY, *as if embarrassed to be so aggressive in front of him.*)

LILLIAN: Do you ever stop asking questions?

RAYMOND: What do you mean?

LILLIAN: There you are. I noticed it before. It's a technique. You don't say anything. You just ask questions.

(*She goes and sits down on a bench which is by the park railings.* RAYMOND *stays where he is, standing.*)

So if the other person's just . . . that little bit less confident than you are . . . they end up talking all the time.

RAYMOND: Mmm.

(*He nods towards the* STABLE BOY.)

Can we let Alistair go?

LILLIAN: (*Angry*) I don't know.

(*Then arbitrarily*) No!

RAYMOND: Are you asking me in?

LILLIAN: No, I'm not.

RAYMOND: What are you doing?

LILLIAN: Sitting here.

(RAYMOND *shrugs slightly at the* STABLE BOY.)

RAYMOND: I want to take Heartfree to the country tomorrow. I was rather hoping you'd come.

LILLIAN: I can't come.

RAYMOND: Why not?

LILLIAN: I have a job.

RAYMOND: What job?

LILLIAN: You see! More questions!

(*He looks a little sheepish.*)

What is *your* job?

RAYMOND: Entrepreneur.

LILLIAN: What on earth does that mean?

RAYMOND: I buy and sell.

(LILLIAN *looks up. The group of girls are now hanging out of the window of the third-floor flat, fully made up for the photographic shoot, laughing hysterically and waving like mad. They are wearing mad, modern clothes, go-go bra tops with tassles, and knitted skirts.* AMY *calls across the street.*)

22

AMY: Are you all right?

LILLIAN: Yes, I'm fine.

AMY: Do you need anything?

LILLIAN: Do you think you could bring some coffee down here?

EXT. HEATH. NIGHT

LILLIAN *and* RAYMOND *are strolling on the heath together. They are coming along a path, through trees,* RAYMOND *holding a thermos in one hand,* LILLIAN *with a plastic cup from which she occasionally drinks. She is still in her dressing gown and jeans. They are quite relaxed.*

RAYMOND: I think the problem is people don't go after things. Or rather, they don't know what it is they want. They don't bother to work out what's important.

LILLIAN: Perhaps most people don't know.

RAYMOND: Well, I know. I've known since childhood.
(*Smiles.*) I saw you in the church. Since then my life has been changed.
(*She is looking down, does not acknowledge this at all. They come to a bench where they sit.*)
We're not here for long. It's so short. My father died . . .

LILLIAN: I'm sorry.

RAYMOND: . . . just recently. It made me understand. It doesn't much matter what the decencies are.
(LILLIAN *frowns.*)

LILLIAN: Yes, but . . . you just get what you want because – let's face it – you have a lot of money . . .

RAYMOND: Agh, money.

LILLIAN: Oh, yeah? Says you, who have it.

RAYMOND: I have it because I think it's nothing. I don't think about it.
(LILLIAN *looks at him a moment.*)

LILLIAN: Mmm, perhaps. Maybe you've just been lucky so far.
(*She gets up and throws the dregs of her coffee into the bushes.*)

RAYMOND: So what do you go after?

LILLIAN: Me?
(*She thinks a moment, as if the question has never occurred to her.*)
I have no idea.

(*She turns suddenly.*)
Well, this is very nice, but I have to be at the hospital in the morning. What time is it?

RAYMOND: Three.

LILLIAN: My God! And where are we? I'm going to have to get home.
(*She laughs, looking round the deserted heath.* RAYMOND *gets up, serious.*)

RAYMOND: May I ring you?

LILLIAN: No. I'll ring you.

RAYMOND: You don't have my number.
(*He gets a gold pen out, then looks for a piece of paper. She holds out her wrist.*)

LILLIAN: Here. You can write it on my hand.
(*He writes his phone number in ballpoint on her hand.*)

INT. LILLIAN'S FLAT. NIGHT

AMY *is lying in bed, her eyes open. Light from the street falls across the bed which is otherwise dark.* LILLIAN *appears in her dressing gown from her room.*

LILLIAN: Amy. I can't sleep.

AMY: What's wrong?

LILLIAN: I don't know.
> (*She sits on the side of the bed.*)
> I'm disturbed.
> (*They both laugh at how absurd this sounds.*)

AMY: You miss Tom?

LILLIAN: Tom? No, of course not. Tom was a loafer. (*Frowns.*) I can't remember. Do you have loafers in America?

AMY: I liked him. Sure, he was dull, but he was romantic. You told me he made love in a bed.
> (LILLIAN *smiles, nostalgically.*)

LILLIAN: Yes.
> (*Then, from down the corridor, the sound of movement in the flat.* LILLIAN *turns, alert, scared.*)
> There's someone out there.

AMY: Oh, it's Carlos.
> (LILLIAN *notices now a pair of jeans at the end of the bed.*)

LILLIAN: Carlos?
> (AMY *nods, looking at* LILLIAN, *who is suddenly terribly sad, having so needed her sister's company.*)
> I should go back to my room.

EXT. STREET. DAY

RAYMOND *pays off a taxi and turns to walk purposefully towards the outside of the hospital.*

EXT. HOSPITAL LOBBY. DAY

At once we see RAYMOND *sitting by himself on a chair in the lobby area, where other patients are ranged until doctors arrive. He is immaculately dressed, and in his hand he has an envelope. On a chair next to him is a large spray of flowers, and a small box, with a gold bow. He has a look of utter contentment on his face, as he waits.*

> *Then suddenly* LILLIAN *is standing in front of him.*

LILLIAN: What is this? A siege?

RAYMOND: Certainly.

LILLIAN: Are you going to lie in wait every hour of the day?

(RAYMOND *has got up and is handing her the envelope.*)

RAYMOND: I want you to read this.

LILLIAN: Oh, yes? Right now?

(*She looks down. It's not sealed. She opens the back of it. There's a folded form inside. The* STAFF NURSE *has appeared and is hovering, waiting for* LILLIAN. *Meanwhile* RAYMOND *is frowning at a man in the next chair who is a very bad colour.*)

STAFF NURSE: Dr Hempel.

LILLIAN: I'm coming.

(*She reads for a moment, then looks at* RAYMOND, *unfazed.*) What on earth makes you think I'd get married in Wandsworth?

RAYMOND: Wandsworth? What's the difference?

(*He leans in confidentially, very worried, as if by something more puzzling.*)

That man's very ill, you know.

LILLIAN: Well, yes. This *is* a hospital.

(*She looks at him in astonishment, but he is already on to the next thing.*)

RAYMOND: There's a taxi waiting.

LILLIAN: I'm beginning to get the hang of your style.

INT. HOSPITAL LOBBY. DAY

They are walking quickly through the busy lobby of the hospital, roaring with laughter, he carrying the flowers and the box. It is exceptionally busy with trolleys going by, wheelchairs, patients, doctors, visitors, cleaners.

LILLIAN: I don't know what made you think I would do it.

(*A* NURSE *approaches to speak to* LILLIAN, *but, anticipating before she can even speak,* LILLIAN *smiles at her.*)

Could you just give me a moment?

(*The* NURSE *is left standing.*)

RAYMOND: You will do it.

LILLIAN: No, well, you're wrong.

RAYMOND: I bet no one's ever asked you.

LILLIAN: How dare you?

(*They grin.*)

26

A boy asked me in Virginia. Not all that long ago. Well, at
least, when I was sixteen.
RAYMOND: So what's your objection? I suppose you don't
believe in it.
LILLIAN: I hardly know you. That's my objection. I could go
further. But it might hurt you.
RAYMOND: Please.
(*She stops. They have reached a row of consulting rooms, all
with doors giving on to the corridor. She suddenly becomes
tactful, as if aware that under the game he has real feelings.*)
LILLIAN: I'm not in love.
RAYMOND: Not yet. Not quite. That will follow.
LILLIAN: Perhaps.
(*He is very still, as if holding his breath. The two of them alone
in the busy corridor. She looks down, as if this were hard to
say.*)
But it's a bit of a risk.
(*He nods as if this is what he had been expecting. At once her
bleeper goes off. Without thinking she turns away and heads for
a phone opposite her office.*)
Excuse me.

INT. CONSULTING ROOM. DAY
RAYMOND *looks round her room, taking in the details of her life,
the institutional bareness, the abandoned books and meals. Then he
looks to the phone, where he can see her talking. After a moment,
she returns.*
RAYMOND: So this is where you work . . .
(LILLIAN *looks at him struck by his quietness.*)
LILLIAN: That was a patient.
RAYMOND: What was wrong?
LILLIAN: What was wrong?
(*She looks at him a moment.*)
He'd had a minor haemorrhage.
RAYMOND: Do you have to go?
LILLIAN: No. I said no. If you go every time you start to get
too emotionally involved. There has to be a limit. It's
actually in everyone's interest. You have to do the job to
the best of your ability and then go on to a life of your
own.

28

(*He is nodding, as if considering this carefully. She stops suddenly, as if also forced to think about what she has just said.*)

RAYMOND: Well, my point exactly. I wonder, what life do you have? Except avoiding your bleeper?

(*He nods at the little black gadget on the desk. Next to it is a plate of two congealed fried eggs with a mound of mashed potato and ketchup on it. He tips the plate slightly towards her. It has long gone cold. She looks up. Through the open door, she can see a group of nurses waiting to speak to her.*)

LILLIAN: Is the taxi still waiting? Let's drive around.

EXT. WIMBLEDON COMMON. DAY

The CAB DRIVER *asleep in his cab. His engine is off. The flowers lie on the seat beside him. Near by, a group of dogs are playing, sniffing each other's bottoms, then running around wild with excitement. Beyond, on a wall,* LILLIAN *is sitting with* RAYMOND. *It looks like deep countryside – a ring of trees and bushes, green stretching away without a building in sight.*

LILLIAN: I wish I didn't feel you understood me. You seem to know what I'm thinking.

RAYMOND: Surely that's a good thing.

(LILLIAN *looks away, not answering.*)

I do understand you. All your life you have to make judgements, you have to be professional and capable and reserved. You have to hold your own life at arm's length. And yet all the time, inside, you want to say yes to something.

LILLIAN: It's not as simple as that.

(*He knows he has reached her. He is very quiet.*)

RAYMOND: You know, you can see, in me there's this terrible stubbornness. When I have an idea. And I have an idea that you are a uniquely interesting and valuable woman. I'm totally in love with you. And I'm old enough to know that I always will be.

(*She turns and looks at him. He is peaceful, simple, inspired.*)

It's not just me. You're ready. For once, to do something. Something which doesn't entirely make sense. To do it and see what happens.

(*He looks at her. Then reaches out his hand and touches the end*

29

*of her hair, by her neck. Instinctively she moves her cheek so
that it rubs softly against his hand. There's a pause.*)

LILLIAN: Also . . . somehow . . . I feel I'm wrongly dressed.

(There's no reaction from him. Or if there is, we don't see it.)

RAYMOND: Mmm.

(He slips quietly down from the wall.)

(Almost inaudibly) I don't want to be late.

INT. WANDSWORTH TOWN HALL. DAY

*A pompous, civic corridor. A bench opposite a closed door. An air of
self-important hush, as in the law courts. As* RAYMOND *and*
LILLIAN *approach, a large Hungarian woman with jet-black hair
and a fur coat rises to embrace* RAYMOND. *She is* JULIA KOVAGO,
early forties.

JULIA: Darling, you're late.

RAYMOND: I was hoping to do it at two thirty. But she took
longer than I thought.

(He smiles easily at LILLIAN, *who stands a little nervous, as*
JULIA's *husband,* IMRE, *approaches from the other direction,
also in his fifties, heavily built, with a bald head and a thick
mohair coat.)*

IMRE: Everything's all right. I've talked to the Registrar.

RAYMOND: This is Imre and Julia Kovago. Lillian.

30

(*They all smile.* JULIA *and* IMRE *turn to go on down the corridor.* LILLIAN *frowns and whispers to* RAYMOND.)

LILLIAN: Who are they?

RAYMOND: Why, they're witnesses, of course.

INT. WANDSWORTH TOWN HALL. DAY

Later. They are all sitting on the bench waiting, LILLIAN *and* RAYMOND *together.* IMRE *and* JULIA *a few feet away. A couple of civil servants go by.* LILLIAN *speaks unexpectedly.*

LILLIAN: What d'you mean, 'buy and sell'?

RAYMOND: What?

LILLIAN: When you said that was your profession?

RAYMOND: I'm a dealer. Mostly in bullion. But I also do
    stocks. And the money market.

LILLIAN: Do you go in to work?

    (RAYMOND *frowns, puzzled.*)

    Do you leave the house?

RAYMOND: Look, let's talk about it later, OK?

    (*At once the door opposite opens. Inside we glimpse briefly a couple standing in front of the desk, kissing. From the room comes the* REGISTRAR, *followed by four policemen.*)

REGISTRAR: I wonder if you would mind waiting. The
    bridegroom is a prisoner. They've just let him out for forty

31

minutes. We thought we should let them have a few
moments alone.

(LILLIAN *looks at the door as it closes on the couple inside.*)

INT. WANDSWORTH TOWN HALL. DAY
*There is now a queue for the Registry Office. Two more wedding
parties have arrived, much more dressed for the occasion – with
bridesmaids in matching suits, bouquets, families, etc.* LILLIAN *is
sitting in the same place, disturbed. The policemen nod at each other,
to show time is up, and slip into the room.*
IMRE: How long is he in prison for?
JULIA: They said seven years.
    (*At once the door is opened and the* PRISONER *is bundled out.
    He is wearing a grey suit and he is handcuffed to one of the
    four policemen who whisk him away, he is crying. The*
    PRISONER'S BRIDE *follows, in floods of tears, on a
    policeman's arm. She is crying uncontrollably.*)
REGISTRAR: Now, Mr Forbes, Miss Hempel, this way.
    (*He gestures towards the door.* LILLIAN *gets up and runs away
    down the corridor as fast as she can.*)
RAYMOND: Lillian!

INT. COUNCIL CHAMBER. DAY
LILLIAN *has run into the big council chamber, bashing the doors
open violently. She sits on one of the great circular benches,
breathing deeply for fresh air.* RAYMOND *follows, stands by the
door.*
LILLIAN: I'm not a *thing*. I can't be treated as if I were a thing.
    As if you were buying me.
RAYMOND: That's not what I feel.
LILLIAN: I'm not getting married. Please don't ask me again.
    (*He looks down, a little shamed.*)
    I will . . . if you like . . . I will live with you.
    (*There's a pause.*)
    Well?

INT. MEWS HOUSE. NIGHT
*The upper level of a mews house. Upstairs, there is an open area
which has a large walk-in wardrobe. The walls are painted a
modish grey, and the whole floor is carpeted in a uniform grey.*

LILLIAN *is running her hand along a line of identical suits. She frowns. Then she looks at shelves of identical white shirts. She frowns. Then she comes towards the spiral staircase which leads downstairs.*

 Downstairs is almost identical. A table, some soft grey chairs, another grey sofa, some piles of magazines. RAYMOND *is standing, thinking, at the far side of the room.*

LILLIAN: I don't get it. Who are you, Raymond? (*Gestures round the room.*) What do you believe?

RAYMOND: I don't believe in sex outside marriage.
 (*She smiles and goes back to the spiral staircase. She goes up it. He follows.*)

LILLIAN: Well, you're just going to have to throw your principles away.
 (*She puts her arm around his waist. From on high the camera swoops down behind them so we are close to their backs as they approach the bedroom. They go in and close the door, even as we move towards them.*
 Fade to black.)

33

PART THREE

EXT. NEWMARKET GALLOPS. DAWN

The early morning mist over Newmarket. Rising from the ground like a thick white layer of smoke. Trees behind. Racing along the gallops comes LILLIAN *on top of a fine chestnut horse, going at full belt along the early morning turf. Then we see the whole sight of Newmarket Down, dozens of horses out exercising, free, fast, easy in the mist.*

EXT. STABLE YARD. DAY

LILLIAN *coming into the stable yard where the horse is taken from her by a boy. There are other horses being taken out for exercise. She dismounts, exhilarated. Waiting is a strange group:* RAYMOND, *in a suit as ever,* IMRE *in a camelhair coat, and* JULIA *done up to the nines, as if about to go night-clubbing.*

LILLIAN: Oh, it's wonderful. It's absolutely wonderful.

RAYMOND: There you are, Imre.

IMRE: That's what her jockey said when she won the
Cheltenham Gold Cup.
(LILLIAN *shakes her head, as a blanket is thrown over the
horse's steaming side.*)
I had such a horse before. Years ago. In Hungary.
JULIA: He did. He had forests. We were happy.
(LILLIAN *leans in to* RAYMOND.)
LILLIAN: It's not like a horse. It's a completely different
thing.
(*A group of horses thunder away into the distance.*)

INT. MARQUEE. DAY
LILLIAN *and* RAYMOND *are in a deserted beer tent, hard by the
race track. He is hunkered down, pouring coffee from a flask.
LILLIAN is still flushed from her ride, exhilarated.*
LILLIAN: Don't you want to ride?
RAYMOND: I like watching you.
(*He hands her coffee.*)
LILLIAN: You can't just *watch*. Don't you have pleasures of
your own?
RAYMOND: Oh, me?
(*He smiles and looks down, as if he were an embarrassing
subject.*)
LILLIAN: Yes.
RAYMOND: Of course.
LILLIAN: Like what?
(*He looks at her a moment, as if judging whether to be
intimate.*)
RAYMOND: Anticipation.
(LILLIAN *frowns a little.*)
I like that feeling when – oh, you know, you're sitting in a
café, you have a glass of wine, you're sitting, you're waiting
for the girl. You think: soon she will join me. It's certain. I
love that feeling of soon she will come.
(LILLIAN *blushes and smiles.* RAYMOND *smiles too.*)
Yes, that also.
(*They sit a moment. They are very happy. Then* LILLIAN
frowns again.)
LILLIAN: But is thinking of things always better than doing
them?

36

RAYMOND: Not always. Hardly. In your case, no.

INT. HOTEL ROOM. EVENING

LILLIAN *is lying back on the bed. She has just bathed
and her hair is wet, combed back from her face. She is wearing a
light silk dressing gown, and looking with an open, easy
fondness across the room to where* RAYMOND *is sitting in just
shirt and trousers, making a note in his diary. He becomes aware of
her look.*

RAYMOND: What are you doing?

    (LILLIAN *does not answer. She just stares, a long penetrating
    look, level, unchanging.* RAYMOND *smiles.*)

LILLIAN: Just watching.

    (*She moves across the room and kisses him.*)

You're not like anyone I know.

    (*He looks up at her, trusting.*)

Because you don't have any cynicism.

RAYMOND: No. None at all.

    (*They hold each other's gaze.*)

INT. CASINO. NIGHT

*The racing party has gone on to the casino. Seated round the roulette
wheel, in evening dress, we recognize* LILLIAN, IMRE, JULIA *and
two businessmen, but the party seems to have enlarged to include
some other conspicuously rich women, and more middle-aged men.
The casino is more like a pretend living room with sofas, silks,
dressings, lampshades: a business pretending to be an upper-class
drawing room. A Cambridgeshire croupier speaks impeccable
French.* LILLIAN, *fresh from the previous scene, is radiant with
happiness.*

CROUPIER: *Faîtes vos jeux*, ladies and gentlemen.

    (LILLIAN *smiles at* JULIA.)

It's spinning.

    (*Meanwhile,* RAYMOND *has just visited the hall, and comes
    back into the main room. He crosses the room and leans over
    * LILLIAN, *who has a small pile of chips in front of her. He puts
    his hand on her shoulder.*)

RAYMOND: How well are you doing?

LILLIAN: I'm going great.

    (*The* CROUPIER *is taking in bets. At the last moment,*

37

RAYMOND *gets a few high-count chips from his pocket and slips them to* LILLIAN.)

RAYMOND: Put a thousand on eight.

LILLIAN: What?

RAYMOND: Will you do it, please?

(*The* CROUPIER *looks expectantly. Just in time,* LILLIAN *frowns and pushes the chips on to eight. The ball spins.* RAYMOND *smiles at* LILLIAN, *unworried. The ball stops on*

22. RAYMOND *shows no reaction at all. Then he sees that*
IMRE *has noticed his loss.* LILLIAN *looks up between them,*
concerned. RAYMOND *speaks quietly.*)
Ah, well, next time.

INT. HOTEL ROOM. DAY
RAYMOND *slips back in the main door of their hotel room.*
His suitcase is already packed on the bed, and LILLIAN
is now packing hers next to it, hurriedly throwing her riding things
in.
LILLIAN: We've got to get going. I'm due back on duty at
  twelve.
RAYMOND: Uh-huh.
  (*She goes to get her last things from the bathroom.* RAYMOND
  frowns, as he calls through.)
  There's a problem. It's just . . . for the moment I can't
  leave.
  (*She comes back with toilet things which she puts in and shuts*
  up the case.)
  It seems a cheque bounced in the casino. They do an early
  call on the bank. And I stupidly gave them one from a
  wrong account.
LILLIAN: You can use a credit card.
RAYMOND: No, they don't take them.
  (*She takes her case from the bed and goes to put it outside*
  the door for the porter. She opens the door. Two men are
  standing outside. They are leaning against the wall, both
  in suits.)
LILLIAN: Ah. Oh, I see.
  (*She closes the door.*)
RAYMOND: I've got someone coming up from London with
  cash. You go back and I'll join you.
LILLIAN: Don't be ridiculous. I'll write a cheque.
  (*She has sat down at the small desk and got out a cheque book*
  from her handbag. Now she looks up at him, as if determined
  not to show the slightest sign of doubt about his trustworthiness.)
RAYMOND: No. Honestly, I don't think you should be paying.
LILLIAN: How much?
RAYMOND: I lost five thousand. Do you have that?
LILLIAN: Well, only just. But you can borrow it.

39

RAYMOND: Thanks.
(*Her hand, moving along the cheque book, writing out in large letters 'Five thousand pounds'.*)
LILLIAN: And then we can leave.

INT. HOSPITAL CORRIDOR. DAY
A sudden panic in the hospital corridor. MR CLARK's *bed is being wheeled at high speed down the corridor. He can be heard protesting, but the* STAFF NURSE *is trying to reassure him. As the bed goes by,* ROMAINE SALMON *flattens herself against the wall, as* LILLIAN *appears round the corner.*
LILLIAN: What's going on?
ROMAINE: It's Mr Clark. He's very upset.
LILLIAN: Ah, yes.
ROMAINE: He's had a lot of trouble since we moved him on to chemotherapy.
(*She looks a moment at* LILLIAN.)
It's a very high dose.
LILLIAN: What do you think? Too high?
ROMAINE: He was losing bladder control. The paralysis is spreading. But we could reduce the dosage. If we're not winning.

INT. MR CLARK'S ROOM. DAY
MR CLARK *is crying in the bed. He is on a drip of Methotrexate from a large yellow bag.* LILLIAN *is sitting on the side. The* STAFF NURSE *stands a few paces off.*
LILLIAN: Now, Mr Clark, it's all right. We did warn you of the side-effects.
MR CLARK: I just hadn't seen.
LILLIAN: I know.
(*He turns. He has lost most of his hair.*)
MR CLARK: I hadn't seen what happened. I'm vomiting all night. All day.
LILLIAN: I know. Nurse, could you please get Mr Clark a cup of tea?
(*She speaks as if angry at the inadequacy of this. Then she puts a hand on his shoulder.*)
We're giving you the best things we have.

40

(She waits a moment. She is being as convincing as she knows how, yet we sense the effort.)
Just trust us. We'll see you through.

INT. LILLIAN'S FLAT. NIGHT
LILLIAN *is standing in the near-dark, the door of her bedroom open in front of her. There is almost no light inside.*
LILLIAN: Amy? Amy? Where are you?
(AMY stirs in Lillian's bed.)
AMY: Is that you, Lillian? What time is it?
LILLIAN: Eight. In the evening.
(She turns on the bedroom light. AMY is like a rat curled up in the crumpled bed. Around her is indescribable chaos of clothes, rucksacks, discarded washing. All the neat cosiness of the room has gone, so that it now looks like a tramp's store room.)
AMY: I took over your bedroom. I thought you were living with that friend of yours.
LILLIAN: Yes. I can see.

INT. LILLIAN'S SITTING ROOM. NIGHT
LILLIAN *is sitting, going through her mail at the table. Around her*

*in the sitting room, things are pretty much the same – the remains
of the photographic sessions, meals, ashtrays, bottles, discarded
clothes. It looks like hell.* AMY *stands at the bedroom door, in
improvised clothing – some wildly inappropriate summer shorts and
a shirt.*

LILLIAN: You said you'd send the mail on.

AMY: Yeah, I meant to.

LILLIAN: What happened to the cleaner?

AMY: Oh, yeah, I let her go.

(*She picks her way through the room towards her cigarettes.*)

LILLIAN: You lost her?

AMY: It's just she always woke me with the vacuum.

(*The mail's going into piles. Now* LILLIAN *throws one angrily
down.*)

LILLIAN: Look, how long since this came?

(AMY *just looks at* LILLIAN *as she picks up a sheaf of notes.*)
What are these?

AMY: Messages.

LILLIAN: Who for?

AMY: Well, for you.

(*She is beginning to sound aggrieved. She looks at her
cigarettes, but then puts them down, rejecting them.*)
It's so long since you were here.

LILLIAN: I left you my number.

AMY: Yeah. I mislaid it. How is . . .

(*She can't remember his name.* LILLIAN *snarls it out angrily.*)

LILLIAN: Raymond? Raymond is fine.

INT. LILLIAN'S KITCHEN. NIGHT

LILLIAN *opens the fridge. It is full of abandoned meals, open tins,
decayed cheese and pickles, little silver packages of dead food. She
stands looking in, quite still.* AMY *appears quietly in the doorway.*

AMY: I didn't tell you. I'm pregnant.

(LILLIAN *doesn't move. She's quiet.*)

LILLIAN: When?

AMY: Oh, you know. About three months ago.

(LILLIAN *closes the fridge door and turns cold, towards her.*)

LILLIAN: Why didn't you call me?

(AMY *doesn't answer.*)
Who's the father?

AMY: Carlos. He's the Argentinian. He's gone to Argentina.
(LILLIAN *looks at her pitilessly.* AMY *looks down.*)
His dad has a ranch.
LILLIAN: What are you going to do?
(AMY *frowns.*)
AMY: Do? I'm not going to do anything.
(LILLIAN *walks silently past her back into the sitting room. As she goes,* AMY *adds:*)
I'm going to sit here and I'm going to give birth.

INT. LILLIAN'S SITTING ROOM. NIGHT
Continuous. LILLIAN *comes through first, cold and quiet.* AMY
follows, trying to be airy, but aware of LILLIAN's *disapproval.*
AMY: Yeah, I've been reading these pamphlets. Cos you work in
regular medicine, I know you won't approve. But I've
found a guy who's just fantastic, in Hampstead. You have
it in a jacuzzi. And they play Mozart. So the child's first
experience is of something beautiful.
(LILLIAN *nods.*)
LILLIAN: Oh, sure. Or else it drowns.
(AMY *looks at her straight across the room.*)
AMY: What's wrong?
(LILLIAN *stares at her, furious.*)
You're angry.
LILLIAN: I'm not angry.
(LILLIAN *suddenly turns, absolutely furious.*)
Have a child? Are you nuts?
AMY: Why not? Why shouldn't I?
LILLIAN: Amy, for God's sake, if you don't understand! Look!
(*She gestures round the room. Then picks up a pair of jeans
which are draped on a chair and throws them down arbitrarily
somewhere else.*)
AMY: Well?
LILLIAN: It's not *you.*
AMY: What is me, for Christ's sake?
LILLIAN: I'll tell you what's you.
(*She picks up an open can of beans which is on the sideboard
and empties them all over the carpet.*)
AMY: Lillian!
LILLIAN: It's beans. It's cans of beans left standing.

43

AMY: For God's sake . . .

LILLIAN: Do you have any idea . . . Jesus Christ, do you know
what's involved?
(*She stands, really furious, her hands on her hips in the middle
of the room.*)

AMY: Yes, I do.

LILLIAN: A child! You've spent your life doing nothing.
Fashion!
(*She picks up a fashion magazine and flings it across the room
in inarticulate anger.*)
What is this? Is this the latest thing? You can't sew a
button! What will you do? Go to college? They don't give
diplomas for dreaming. Let alone diplomas for fucking!
Let's face it, you've had a free ride. Who'll look after it?
Me. Thank you! While you dance around London with
your friends, talking about how one day you're going to
make a dress.

AMY: Is that what will happen?

LILLIAN: Well, I mean, I'm just going on past record . . .

AMY: I don't have it in me?
(LILLIAN *just looks at her.*)
What, you think people can't change?
(LILLIAN *does not reply.*)
Lillian?
(*She is suddenly very quiet and serious.*)
Can they? Please tell me. Can they?
(LILLIAN *shifts uneasily.*)

LILLIAN: Look, I don't want to seem cruel . . .

AMY: No. Of course you're not cruel. Oh, of course, you're the
kind one, I was told that – fuck! – from the moment I was
born . . .

LILLIAN: Amy . . .

AMY: You were the one who could do everything and be nice to
everyone. And I was the ditzy little scrag of a sister who
couldn't be trusted to tie her own shoes.

LILLIAN: I never said that.

AMY: But that's what you think. That's how you see me.
(*Smiles.*) Oh, you're always so kind. So patient. So tolerant.
And in that kindness, doctor, there's such condescension.

44

(LILLIAN *looks mistrustfully from the other side of the room,*
silenced. AMY *is very calm.*)
You know what I think? I'm going to see it through. And
you don't like it. Why? Because I think you're jealous.
(AMY *looks at her a moment, then she turns and goes back very*
quietly into the bedroom. LILLIAN *is left sitting alone.*)

INT. COLIN'S HOUSE. NIGHT
At once the sound of rock music, beating away in a darkened sitting
room. COLIN *lives in a very small house in South London, of*
conventional suburban design, which he shares with three other
young doctors. He is giving an incredibly loud and noisy party.
A table of drink has been set up in the hallway where it serves to
block the entrance to the sitting room. LILLIAN *has just arrived*
and is pushing her way through the crowd in the hall to COLIN
who is coming from the sitting room, very drunk. He's wearing
a kilt.
LILLIAN: Colin, good to see you.
COLIN: Lillian, darling!
    (*He stumbles and at once falls out of frame.* SABOLA *has*
    appeared beside LILLIAN, *carrying five glasses of wine. He*
    gives two to LILLIAN. *They have to shout, their faces very*
    close, the room full of dancers immediately in front of them.)
SABOLA: Colin hardly knows what's happening.
LILLIAN: Well, I can see that.
SABOLA: He's dancing to oblivion.
    (LILLIAN *takes* SABOLA'*s arm.*)
LILLIAN: We can't let him go there alone.
    (SABOLA'*s drink spills.*)

INT. COLIN'S SITTING ROOM. NIGHT
The small suburban sitting room is a riot of people dancing, the
whole room one pumping mass. LILLIAN *is bopping with* SABOLA,
and they both have lots of energy. ROMAINE *is dancing wildly*
nearby them, the centre of attraction. Suddenly there is a shouting for
silence. COLIN *is getting up on a table.*
COLIN: Quiet please, everyone. There are going to be *games.*
    (*A lot of cheering. The music is turned down.*)

We are going to play the Rice Krispies game.
(*More cheering.*)
And everyone – please – first prize: you get to look up my
kilt.
(*This brings the house down. Mass cheering.*)

INT. COLIN'S HALL. NIGHT
*From the hall we see a crowd gathered round a couple of nurses who
are playing a game with blindfolds and spoons of Rice Krispies.
Cascades of breakfast cereal fall from spoons down cleavages, to
hysterical laughter all round.* LILLIAN, *holding a drink above her
head, pushes her way through shouting back at* SABOLA *who is
following her.*

LILLIAN: I don't know what it is about doctors. You think
    they'd get enough of it at work. But when they get home
    all they want to do is look at each other's genitals.
    (SABOLA *nods in agreement, laughing. In the distance the low
    front of one of the women's dresses is pulled down and Rice
    Krispies cascade down her breasts.*)
    I mean, fishmongers don't go home and look at fish.
    (LILLIAN *heads for the front door to get home, but* ROMAINE
    is waiting to intercept her with mock casualness.)
ROMAINE: Lillian, please, you're not going . . .
LILLIAN: Oh, Romaine . . .
ROMAINE: I'm sorry. You did say you'd talk.
LILLIAN: Yes. It's my fault. *I'm* sorry. I've just had no time.
    (LILLIAN *smiles at her.* ROMAINE *waits.*)
    I hope you saw I signed the petition.
ROMAINE: To be honest I hoped you'd do much more.
LILLIAN: I see that. But the fact is I am American. It does
    make a difference. I don't mean to sound uncaring but in a
    way it isn't my fight.
    (ROMAINE *looks at her, controlling her anger.*)
ROMAINE: Lillian, we've lost forty beds. Three specialties are
    now under threat of permanent closure from chronic
    underfunding. All right, it's a scandal. Everyone agrees.
    Yet I can't find one doctor above the rank of junior
    registrar willing to head a properly organized, high-profile
    public protest. Which might actually be at some personal
    cost.

46

(LILLIAN *begins to lose patience.*)

LILLIAN: I know, but it's all so English. For God's sake, what is this party for? Colin has already been sacked. It's too late.

(*She suddenly lets fly at* ROMAINE, *with a burst of unsuspected anger.*)

If you wanted to fight, why didn't you fight effectively?

(*She reaches angrily for the front door. But she gets the wrong one. It's the bathroom. Inside,* HELEN, *the nurse, has her skirt round her waist. A young man is making love to her against the wall.*)

ROMAINE: That's not the . . .

(*But* LILLIAN *has already seen.*)

LILLIAN: I'm sorry, nurse.

INT. MEWS SITTING ROOM. NIGHT

LILLIAN *is sitting alone on the grey sofa in the grey sitting room. She is reading a book. Then down on the table beside her a hand puts five thousand pounds in notes. On top is a glistening silver bracelet.*

LILLIAN: What's this?

(*She looks up.* RAYMOND *has come in and put the money down beside her, unobserved. He's smiling.*)

RAYMOND: Your money. With interest. I'm afraid I had to get it in cash.

(*She lifts the bracelet and puts it to one side.*)

LILLIAN: I don't need gifts.

(*He kneels down in front of her.*)

RAYMOND: Are you all right?

LILLIAN: I'm frightened. It's what you once said. Time's going so fast.

(*He puts his head in her lap. But after a moment she gets up and crosses the room.*)

I had a row with Amy. I realized I'm getting kind of angry. She said I had no courage. That I never did anything brave.

RAYMOND: That's not true.

LILLIAN: Well, in a way it is. And, with you, it occurred to me, it took me so long to trust you. I just thought today, you know what lies ahead? Going through all

that endless process, building this thing up. Painfully.
Man–woman, that kind of stuff. Why? It's ridiculous.
After all, I know what I feel. For once in my life, let's
jump the stages.
(*He looks up, moved.*)
Do you still have the licence?
(*He takes the wallet from his pocket. Inside, folded, is the piece
of paper. He unfolds it neatly.*
She smiles.)
Good. Let's cash it in.

INT. REGISTRY OFFICE. DAY
It is deadly quiet. LILLIAN *and* RAYMOND *stand like
schoolchildren in front of the headmaster. There is a simple desk with
the* REGISTRAR *behind it. Behind* LILLIAN *and* RAYMOND,
IMRE *and* JULIA *are sitting on otherwise empty benches, benign but
impenetrable smiles on their faces. There is a silence while the*
REGISTRAR *seems to search for his papers.*
REGISTRAR: No other witnesses?
LILLIAN: None.
(*He looks at them a moment.* RAYMOND *takes the ring from
his pocket.* LILLIAN's *hand as he slips it on her finger. It is all
strangely silent. Then from behind, we see him put his arm
round her.*)

EXT. SEA. NIGHT
The sea at night. Infinite. The moon on water. Still, silent.

INT. HOTEL ROOM. NIGHT
A tiny little silver statue, no more than an inch high, of the horse
LILLIAN *rode on Newmarket Down. It is exquisitely sculptured,
tiny between* RAYMOND's *finger and thumb, as he puts it down on a
bedside table.* LILLIAN *is lying on the hotel bed. Beyond her, the
doors of the veranda are open to the sea beyond. She looks, awed, at
this little piece, drawing her breath in between her teeth. The only
noise but for the distant waves.*
Fade to black.

PART FOUR

INT. RAYMOND'S OFFICES. DAY
We are behind RAYMOND *as we fade up on his back, as he comes down the central corridor of his offices. They are very modern, and there are half-open doors into rooms off the central corridor, but the effect is as if they have only just been moved into. There is a beige carpet, oatmeal walls, and slick frosted glass.* RAYMOND *is carrying his overnight bag as he approaches the main office at the end. It is strangely quiet. At a desk is a secretary called* JILL, *a posh English girl of about twenty-three.*
JILL: Are you Mr Forbes? I'm the new temporary.
RAYMOND: Hello.
  (*She hands him a pile of cables and telexes. There is a fax machine and a topic screen, an electric typewriter, but otherwise the office is almost bare.*)
JILL: All these came. They need an answer in Tokyo. Also these prices came through on the fax, marked very urgent.
  (*She gestures towards a desk full of papers. But* RAYMOND *takes only the first pile offered and carries straight through to his own adjoining office.*)
RAYMOND: Don't worry, I'll deal with it.

INT. RAYMOND'S OFFICE. DAY
Continuous. Equally bare, as if he only just squats there, but framed by a huge window which looks out on to St Paul's Cathedral. RAYMOND *comes through the door and goes round to look at the untouched paperwork on his desk. Then he reaches for a silver frame on the desk. It has a picture of* LILLIAN *in it. He stands looking at it a moment.*

INT. SCRUBBING ROOM. DAY
LILLIAN *is scrubbing away at her hands by a line of basins. She is hurrying.* SABOLA *is a few basins down, scrubbing away.*
SABOLA: You're looking very well.
LILLIAN: Well, thank you, Harold. I'm feeling pretty good.
  (*She turns the taps off with her elbows, not now able to touch anything. Then she frowns, noticing that she has put her*

wedding ring down on the basin, and can't now pick it up.
SABOLA *notices.*)
SABOLA: Have you been off getting married?
LILLIAN: Oh, no. Not at all. Nurse.
(*She nods at the ring to the* NURSE *who is standing waiting with her green gown. The* NURSE *picks it up and slips it into the pocket of her gown.*)
A man just gave me this ring.

INT. HOSPITAL CORRIDOR. DAY
LILLIAN *pads down the corridor to go to the changing room after the operation. She is smiling to herself in the same way she was in the scrubbing room. She is still in her greens, in the empty corridor. Suddenly* HELEN *appears.*
HELEN: Dr Hempel. A Mr Forbes was trying to ring you.
LILLIAN: Ah, yes.
HELEN: He's had to go abroad, but he'll be back soon.
LILLIAN: I'm sorry?
(*But* HELEN *has already run off to attend to a distant patient.*)
HELEN: That was it.
(LILLIAN *alone in the empty corridor.*)
LILLIAN: Thanks.

EXT. MEWS. NIGHT

A silver BMW glides into the mews. The engine has been turned off so that it slips in completely quietly, light playing on its side in the otherwise darkened street. As it draws close, we see RAYMOND's *face at the wheel. He draws the car to a halt. Then he looks across to the mews house. The lights are on inside, and the effect is extraordinarily comforting. Neat, welcoming, cosy.*

We look in close up at RAYMOND's *face. Tears are pouring down his cheeks.*

INT. MEWS SITTING ROOM. NIGHT

LILLIAN *is sitting alone in the mews house. She has a light on over the desk at which she's working. Books, papers, around her.*
RAYMOND *comes in through the front door, leaving it open. There is no trace of his tears.*
RAYMOND: Look. Over there.
> (*She frowns. Then gets up. She walks to the door. Outside, in the cobbled mews there is the BMW. He watches her for a moment.*)
It's a car.
LILLIAN: What d'you mean?
> (*She stands, puzzled. He's holding out the keys to her.*)
RAYMOND: Well, it's just a way of saying . . . I'm sorry I suddenly had to go away. I had to go to Zurich.
> (*She looks at him a moment, then she turns and goes back into the room to sit down again at her desk.*)
I just thought you'd like it. I thought your old one was looking pretty stupid. So I thought you'd like a surprise.
> (*She is looking at him, thinking.*)
Well, I'm back. I booked a special restaurant.
LILLIAN: I don't want to go.
> (*He waits a moment, then closes the front door. He stands, his back to her.*)
You always give me gifts. And take me to restaurants. And send me flowers. As if you're still trying to get me. It doesn't make sense. You've got me.
RAYMOND: Uh-huh.
> (*She looks up at him.*)
LILLIAN: Now I want things *not* to be special. I want them to be ordinary. So let's stay in, and just read a book.

53

(*She returns to her reading.* RAYMOND *stands alone, with a look of total dismay, as if his world has just crashed to the ground. He goes and sits on the sofa, his hands on his knees, doing nothing, thinking, waiting. Then after a few moments he gets up.*)

RAYMOND: I'm going for a walk.

LILLIAN: Look, I'm sorry.

RAYMOND: No, I want to.

LILLIAN: I don't mean to upset you.

(*He is standing beside her. She reaches out and takes his hand.*) It's just we now . . . surely we now want to have some ordinary life. Isn't that right?

(*He doesn't answer.*)

There's got to be a period where we just settle.

RAYMOND: Yes, you're right.

LILLIAN: Surely?

RAYMOND: (*Smiles.*) No, I agree.

(*He sits on the sofa with the most pained expression, things no better. After a while,* LILLIAN *speaks.*)

LILLIAN: We've never had a row.

RAYMOND: Nor shall we.

LILLIAN: Sometimes I think you don't have any skin. You have no defences.

(*He reaches over and kisses her. They kiss for a while. Then he looks at her.*)

RAYMOND: It's just a short walk. I'll be back soon.

(*He holds his face beside hers a moment. She smiles. She reaches up and touches the side of his face. He smiles, turns and goes out.*)

EXT. MEWS. NIGHT

The deserted mews. Nothing moves. The BMW parked directly opposite the door of their house.

EXT. MEWS. NIGHT

LILLIAN *is in her pink dressing gown, as she answers the repeated knocking at her front door. Outside a well-bred middle-aged woman, in coat and dress.*

NEIGHBOUR: Excuse me, is this your car?

54

LILLIAN: You mean, does it belong to me?
NEIGHBOUR: It's blocking my garage. I can't get out.
  (*She gestures to where her own car is blocked by the BMW
  parked directly outside the opposite doors.*)
LILLIAN: Well, actually the keys are with my . . . the man who
  . . . a friend of mine. He should be back, but I'm not too
  sure when.
  (The NEIGHBOUR *walks round as if by looking at it it will
  move.* LILLIAN *joins her thoughtfully, staring at the gleaming
  silver car.*)
NEIGHBOUR: I don't know what to do.
LILLIAN: No, well, I wish I knew how to help.

INT. MEWS BEDROOM. NIGHT
LILLIAN *lies alone in bed, alert. The moonlight falls through the
open window. She is quite still, her eyes gleaming and bright.*

EXT. MEWS. DAY
*Out in the mews the BMW is now being lifted into the air on a
chain mechanism which swings it into the air and lifts it on to the*

back of a truck which has the name of a garage prominent on its side. There is no one else about.

At the bedroom window, seen from the mews, LILLIAN's *face appears, the reality of her fears coming home to her.*

INT. SIMULATOR ROOM. DAY

X-rays up on the light board being examined by MR COOPER. *The morning meeting of the whole cancer team, which numbers about seven, including* ROMAINE *and* SABOLA. *There are radiographers, some in white coats.* MR COOPER *is referring to the X-ray.*

MR COOPER: This is obviously a fellicular lymphatic tumour.
   This is an absolutely classic instance of diagnostic choice.
   We may either attempt total nodal irradiation, or hand the
   patient over to our friends in medical oncology.
   (*He looks across the room to* LILLIAN, *who is sitting by
   herself, staring, outside the X-ray group.*)
   Lillian?
   (*She turns towards him, out of her dream.*)
LILLIAN: What? I'm sorry, Mr Cooper.
   (*She looks round. They are waiting for her verdict.*)
   Give this one back to me. I'll look at it again.

INT. HOSPITAL. DAY

LILLIAN *comes distressed out of the simulator room, and heads back
down the corridor towards her office. From some way off she sees
two men lounging against the door of her room. As she draws closer,
they do not move at all. The first to speak is called* FAULKNER. *He
has a Cockney accent and an off-grey suit with a blue tie. He's
solidly built, about thirty.*

FAULKNER: Miss Hempel? We've met. You remember? In
   Newmarket. I think you opened a door.
   (*She pauses, remembering. The other man,* PEVERILL *just
   watches. He's also thirtyish, but taller, blonder, and very
   large.*)
   We're trying to find Mr Forbes.
LILLIAN: Oh, really? Well, he's been abroad.
   (*The two men look one to another across her.*)
FAULKNER: What, recently?
LILLIAN: Yes. He was in Switzerland . . .
FAULKNER: Ah.

LILLIAN: Earlier this week.
(PEVERILL *has taken a passport from his pocket and is now holding it up.*)
What's that?
FAULKNER: His passport. He lent it to us in Newmarket. As a form of security.
PEVERILL: He has some bad debts.
(LILLIAN *looks at them, then goes into her office, having to pass between them. As she is about to go in* FAULKNER *speaks, still not moving.*)
FAULKNER: Where will you be, Miss Hempel?
LILLIAN: Me?
FAULKNER: You're not thinking of travelling? We will need our money.
(LILLIAN *looks down.*)
LILLIAN: That's not to do with me.
PEVERILL: You're the nearest relative.
LILLIAN: But I'm not a relative.
(*There is a moment as* PEVERILL *casts another glance across to* FAULKNER.)
FAULKNER: No.

INT. MEWS BEDROOM. NIGHT

LILLIAN *sits alone in a darkened room. Night has long come down. She is not moving, just staring. Then she gets up and goes to the window of the bedroom. Outside in the darkened mews* PEVERILL *and* FAULKNER *are standing, still waiting, two dark figures, silent, still.*

INT. RAYMOND'S OFFICES. DAY

LILLIAN *puts the key into the lock of the outer door of Raymond's offices. She opens the door. They are abandoned. As soon as she steps in, she knows there is no one there. She pushes a pile of mail out of the way with the door. Then, hearing the noise of a distant telex machine, she is drawn down the corridor to the main office. She goes in. The telex is chattering to itself in what is otherwise a deserted room. The temp,* JILL, *has gone, leaving her papers just where they were.*

LILLIAN *goes on into Raymond's office. She stands at the door. Everything on the desk is neat. Diaries, books, papers. Then she frowns at the back of the picture frame, which is still on the desk, its face turned away from us.*

Slowly, full of fear, she approaches the desk. Her hand reaches out for the frame. She picks it up and turns it round. It is empty. Her photo has gone.

She looks up.

INT. HOSPITAL. DAY

LILLIAN *is sitting in her office all alone, staring out of the window. Work is piled up hopelessly around her.* ROMAINE *is standing opposite, waiting patiently as* LILLIAN *finally turns towards her.* ROMAINE *has a patient's charts in her hand.*

ROMAINE: Dr Hempel. I'm sorry. It's just . . .

(*She pauses, nervous of* LILLIAN's *mood.*)

LILLIAN: Yes. Go on.

ROMAINE: Mr Cooper's confused by your analysis. On one of this morning's admissions. He believes your dosages are wrong.

(*She waits. But* LILLIAN *just looks at her blankly.* ROMAINE *is fazed. She puts the charts down in front of* LILLIAN *who ignores them.*)

They're wrong.

LILLIAN: Yes, I understand.
  (*She is unnaturally quiet.*)
ROMAINE: Well?
LILLIAN: What? Isn't this why we have a computer?
  (ROMAINE *nods.*)
  Then tell him, please, put the dosages right.
  (*She suddenly gets up and goes out of the room.*)

INT. HOSPITAL LOBBY. DAY
LILLIAN *is moving very quickly down the corridor, struggling to maintain her self-control, biting her lip, looking straight ahead. As she comes to the main lobby, she begins to run, irrationally, nowhere, just to escape, when suddenly* SABOLA *appears in pursuit.*
SABOLA: Lillian, hey, come here. What's happening?
LILLIAN: I'm sorry.
  (*A* NURSE *appears for her, but* LILLIAN *waves her away.*)
NURSE: Dr Hempel?
LILLIAN: I just . . . look, I'm sorry, I do need a break.
  (*From another corridor, another* NURSE *now stands in front of her, blocking her way.*)
SECOND NURSE: Excuse me, I wonder . . .
LILLIAN: No, I can't. All right? I can't. Do you understand?
  (*She is suddenly shouting at the top of her voice at the* NURSE. *Heads turn. The old men, lame women, noisy children, receptionists all turn to look.*)
  Whatever it is. I don't know what it is. But I can't do it.
  (*Suddenly they are all staring at her in the corridor. She looks wildly at them all, trapped.*)
SABOLA: Lillian . . .
LILLIAN: Please, just leave me alone.
  (*Instinctively she turns, and grabs the nearest door, which she wrenches open and then slams shut, leaving the rest of them in the corridor.*)

INT. SUPPLIES CUPBOARD. DAY
The supplies cupboard. There are wooden shelves, not unlike a small sauna. The only light source is a small high window which throws light in a square on LILLIAN'*s face. Dirty laundry is around her on the floor, and on the shelves above her, bottles, swabs, all the*

59

apparatus of the hospital. She is sitting in the very corner, like an animal in a cage. But it's warm in the cupboard, and quite cosy. The door opens, and SABOLA *comes in, gently. He closes the door. She looks up, then runs her hand in front of her face. He is the soul of tact, sympathetic, silent. After a while she speaks.*

LILLIAN: Where am I? You know. Can I ask that? For years I've done nothing but give. Just give. Oh, I know, it's rewarding, of course. But there is something you're not meant to ask.

(SABOLA's *face, looking at her distress with great fondness.*)
The giving's great. It's great. I'm sorry, but when do I get something back?

INT. HOSPITAL CORRIDOR. DAY
Outside in the corridor there is now a disorderly crowd of about twenty-five people. Nurses, auxiliary workers, stray patients. They are all grouped round the cupboard door, waiting. Down the corridor now MR COOPER *is coming, thunder-faced, moving slowly and sombrely towards the scene.*

MR COOPER: In here? I see. Right, everyone. Give Dr Hempel some space.

(*Down the corridor comes the* TEA LADY *with a trolley. Everyone clears.* MR COOPER *waits, then is handed a cup of tea in an institutional green cup.*)
Thank you, everyone. I'm going in.

INT. SUPPLIES CUPBOARD. DAY
MR COOPER *comes silently through the door.* LILLIAN's *face is covered.* SABOLA *looks up. At the sight of* MR COOPER *he slips tactfully out of the door.* MR COOPER *walks across, holding out the tea.*

MR COOPER: I've brought a cup of tea.

(*She takes it, silently.*)
You have to go back to work.

LILLIAN: Yes, Mr Cooper.

(*The atmosphere has changed decisively. She takes a sip.*)

MR COOPER: It's good work. You bring comfort.

(*She looks down a moment.*)

60

You can always have this cupboard. Whenever you need it.
LILLIAN: Thank you.
(*He looks at her, his manner impenetrably sober and serious.*)
MR COOPER: It's yours.

INT. LILLIAN'S BEDROOM. NIGHT
AMY *and* LILLIAN *are sleeping in the same bed.* LILLIAN *is lying in the darkened room, her eyes open.* AMY *lies beside her, ostensibly asleep.* LILLIAN *is staring at the ceiling.*
AMY: Lillian, please sleep.
(LILLIAN *doesn't move.*)
What time is it?
LILLIAN: Every time I turn I bump into your baby.
AMY: Thank you. How do you think I feel?
LILLIAN: It's pointless. I'm not going to sleep.
(*She throws the cover back to get out of bed.* AMY *hoists herself painfully up the bed.*)
I'm lying here getting angry. I don't know if I'm angrier with him or with me.
AMY: It's not your fault if he's gone.
LILLIAN: It turns out he didn't own anything. He was spending

all this money. Which he didn't have. Buying me things. It's just crazy. I told him, I never wanted the stuff. I wanted him.

AMY: Well, sure.

LILLIAN: And now I don't know . . . I've just had enough of it. People were coming to the door. I can see it's irrational, but I decided I'd better pay.

(AMY *is now sitting up in bed.* LILLIAN *is standing by the window now, tears in her eyes.*)

Yes, his debts. I mean only the private ones.

AMY: How much have you spent?

(LILLIAN *turns, slightly hysterical.*)

LILLIAN: I'm a National Health doctor. I've nothing left.

INT. LILLIAN'S SITTING ROOM. NIGHT

Continuous. LILLIAN *comes through into the darkened room, in distress. She sits on the sofa, not turning the light on.* AMY *follows now, out of bed, in a long white T-shirt, which comes down beyond her knees.*

AMY: When did you do this?

LILLIAN: Today, I wrote a lot of cheques. I thought, fuck off, the lot of you. Go away. Leave me. Please. Just leave me.

AMY: It's not too late. The cheques can be stopped.

(LILLIAN *looks at her mercilessly, as if she was a fool. The look provokes* AMY.)

Lillian, they're not your debts. They're nothing to do with you. How long did you know him?

LILLIAN: (*Shaking her head.*) That's not the point. The fact is, I knew.

AMY: What d'you mean?

LILLIAN: I just *knew* . . .

AMY: *What?*

LILLIAN: All the time I was with him, oh, he was always buying me things. Of course I was flattered. I went along with it. But I *knew*. He was running on empty.

(*She turns, shaking her head.*)

That's why I sort of feel in a way it's my fault.

AMY: Lillian, that's crazy.

LILLIAN: He was in love with me.

(*She shouts this at* AMY, *as if it were the ultimate explanation.*
AMY *looks at her a moment, then crosses to pick up Lillian's*
handbag from the table.)

AMY: Find me your cheque book. We'll get the numbers. Then
in the morning I'll ring the bank.

(LILLIAN *doesn't move.*)

LILLIAN: Also, the thing is . . . I did something stupid. Which
I didn't tell you. I married him.

(AMY *turns, from the table, the bag in her hand.*)

AMY: *What?*

(AMY *is suddenly seized with fury at one side of the room.*)
When?

(LILLIAN *snaps at the irrelevance of this question.*)

LILLIAN: *When?* When you weren't looking. The fact is, I felt
wild. I felt old and wild. I was lonely. Shit, I don't know.
Don't look at me like that.

(AMY *is not moving.* LILLIAN *has suddenly shouted. Now she*
quietens and almost pleads with AMY.)

Amy, he went to the heart of me.

AMY: Please.

(AMY *turns away.*)

LILLIAN: Well, it's true.

(AMY *shakes her head, lost for words.*)

AMY: I mean, hell, you know, I mean . . . the life I've been
leading . . . like I've been walking around all this time,
feeling guilty, oh, my God, how can I bring a child into the
world?

LILLIAN: Yeah, I . . .

AMY: You know, I mean, I'm not *worthy*, I don't have the
character. You know, my big sister tells me . . . because
the room isn't neat . . .

(*She suddenly crosses the room and turns the light on.*
Everything is in its place again, neat and tidy.)
Look!

LILLIAN: I saw.

AMY: Because I never see anything through – look – proper
finished designs –

(*She holds up three dress designs, perfectly drawn, fabric*
samples pinned to them, Cellophane wrapped . . .)

LILLIAN: They're great.

AMY: I mean, for months I've been going round on my knees,
licking dust off the carpet . . .
(*She runs a finger along the mantelpiece and holds it up.*)
Polished!

LILLIAN: All right.

AMY: . . . to *prove* to my sister that I'm a suitable person.

LILLIAN: Yeah, I was hideous.

(AMY *is shaking her head.*)

AMY: You made me feel terrible. I've had months of feeling
terrible. And what were you doing meanwhile?
(*She turns and talks to an imaginary person.*)
'I mean, do you know my sister Lillian? Yeah, the doctor.
Yeah. No, she was off, er, well, actually she was, er,
marrying someone. Yeah, without telling us. Mmm. A man
she knew was a *crook.*'

LILLIAN: He's not a crook.

AMY: Then what is he?

LILLIAN: I don't know. If I knew do you think I'd be feeling
like this?
(AMY *relents, touched by* LILLIAN'*s sudden desperation.*)
The fact is, we were in the middle of something. I *know* we
were. I *know* it. I know it was real. And it still goes on.
There's only one difference. (*Pauses, suddenly quiet.*) I'm
still with him. But he isn't there.
(*Fade to black.*)

66

PART FIVE

INT. CHAPEL. DAY

At once Christ again, this time on a stained-glass window. The windows are immensely high, throwing light in dusty diagonals on to the stone floor of a huge Gothic chapel. A man has his back to us, looking up at the window, in rapt contemplation. LILLIAN *is standing a long way behind him, rows and rows of pews stretching away in front of her. She approaches, then speaks very quietly.*

LILLIAN: I'm sorry. I don't mean to disturb you.

(*He turns. He's in his early sixties. He has a sports jacket and striped tie. He has white hair in what remains of a wave, and a tanned face. His name is* DOUGLAS BRODIE.)

BRODIE: There's no problem.

(*He looks puzzled.*)

Are you here already?

LILLIAN: Yes, I'm Lillian Hempel.

BRODIE: Ah, welcome.

(*They shake hands.*)

You don't have to lower your voice. I hate the way people lower their voices in church.

(*He speaks at a normal or above-normal level which seems odd in the religious surroundings.*)

LILLIAN: I just thought I was interrupting.

BRODIE: Good Lord, no. I was just enjoying a reminder. I've lost my faith.

(*Smiles broadly.*)

Yes, I know it's unusual. Most people as they get older tend to run for cover, so to speak. They take out an insurance policy.

(*He gestures her to move on down the church.*)

Well, I decided I'd throw mine away.

EXT. CHAPEL. DAY

They move through the grounds of the chapel, which are very beautiful, the great buttresses behind them, in front of them summer flowers and well-cut lawns.

BRODIE: What, you say he just vanished?

LILLIAN: Yes.

BRODIE: How recently?

LILLIAN: A few weeks ago. It's just he sometimes used to talk
about you. It suddenly occurred to me he might come here.
If he was in trouble.

(BRODIE *shrugs*.)

BRODIE: He never has.

(*They come to some steps leading up to the quadrangle.*
Hundreds of boys in uniform are now running on their way to
class, or standing talking, or kicking footballs, in front of them.
BRODIE *laughs a little*.)

I never seem to see him. He does send us presents.
Ridiculous presents. Once he sent us a sheep.

LILLIAN: He sent me a horse.

BRODIE: A horse? Our sheep was in pieces. For the freezer, I
mean.

(LILLIAN *smiles*.)

LILLIAN: Ah, yes. My horse was alive.

(BRODIE *looks at her mistrustfully a moment, as if trying to*
work her out.)

68

The first time I met him, I said I liked horses. Then a few days later there was one on my doorstep. I was only making conversation. I might have said anything. (*Smiles.*) I might have said I liked *hearses.*
(BRODIE *looks at her disapprovingly.*)
BRODIE: Yes. Then you had a narrow escape.
(*They walk across the quadrangle. The school bell is ringing and the scene clears completely of boys.*)

EXT. CLOISTERS. DAY
They walk on along some medieval cloisters, open to the air.
BRODIE: He was brought up abroad. His mother went off with an unsuitable man. She was killed in an air crash, somewhere inside Venezuela.
LILLIAN: Yes, he said.
BRODIE: His father was distracted; remiss, you would call it. And so it occurred to my wife and me that Raymond could stay with us in the holidays. We had no children. And so we took him into our home.

INT. SCHOOL HALL. DAY
A massive vaulted school hall, immensely large and imposing. Wood-panelled walls. Off it, there are many doors leading to classrooms, now in session. It is absolutely deserted except for a last boy hurrying late into class. BRODIE *and* LILLIAN *walk through.*
LILLIAN: He was here every holiday?
BRODIE: Yes. He was by himself. When the school was empty. He would play with the football on the school grounds.
(*He gestures towards the stage at the end of the hall.*)
Once I found him alone in this place. Practising making a speech.
(*They stop a moment, involuntarily, awed at the idea of a small boy in such a large hall.*)
LILLIAN: What was the speech about?
BRODIE: Dreams.
(LILLIAN *stands a moment, thinking. Then she swings round at the sound of a voice.*)

69

DAPHNE: We want to give you tea.

(*Standing beside her is a fair, distracted woman in her early sixties. She is sensibly dressed in a skirt and cashmere pullover. Some wisps of hair fall across her handsome face. She seems barely present.*)

BRODIE: This is my wife, Daphne.

LILLIAN: Hello.

(*She shakes her hand. They begin to move back towards the door.*)

DAPHNE: Then, darling, remember you have a class.

(LILLIAN *looks a moment between them,* BRODIE *not answering.*)

BRODIE: I worked very hard. For years I tutored him. I got him a scholarship to Oxford. But he never went. He met a girl. You can never rely on him. Eventually he lets everyone down.

(BRODIE *passes out of the hall.* DAPHNE *is holding the hall door open, as* LILLIAN *is about to pass through.*)

DAPHNE: Ignore him.

LILLIAN: I'm sorry?

DAPHNE: Raymond loved women.

(LILLIAN *stops a moment, brought up short. She looks at* DAPHNE, *whose expression is unreadable.*)

LILLIAN: Yes.

DAPHNE: It's very rare.

(LILLIAN *looks at her, taken aback.*)

EXT. COTTAGE. DAY

A cottage in Gloucestershire. The sun is out, beating down on the grey-brick cottage, which is set in the middle of the countryside. All around it is a cultivated area, vegetables, flowers, lawns, but then, without hedges, it merges straight into field and meadow. The front door is open as LILLIAN *approaches, but it appears to be deserted. She begins to walk round. Around the back some chickens are scratching about, with some ducks. Then as she gets nearer, a huge pale brown dog comes running suddenly towards her, cheerfully barking in a friendly sort of way. It sniffs her out, and then at once runs away off into the garden.*

LILLIAN *turns. There's still no one about. Then she sees in the corner of the garden a boy working under a tree. He has his*

70

computer terminal in front of him, and he is frowning at it intently.
He is so absorbed in his work – the table and chair neatly laid out –
that he does not notice LILLIAN.

Then, from the front door of the house comes ANNIE RICE. *She is*
wearing jeans and a shirt. She is in her forties, her face fine and
coloured by fresh air. She is very thin, and carries a trug full of
flowers.

ANNIE: Hello. Are you from the nursery?
LILLIAN: The nursery?
ANNIE: Are you bringing me plants? I'm expecting some
wisteria. Mine's had the blight.
LILLIAN: No.
(ANNIE *gestures towards the plant climbing up the front wall of*
the cottage.)
ANNIE: This summer's been an absolute fucker.
LILLIAN: Yes. I agree with you there.

EXT. COTTAGE. DAY
RICHARD, *who is twelve, working at his computer as the two*
women approach. ANNIE *has put her trug down, and is taking*

71

off her gardening gloves as she calls out to him, LILLIAN
following.

ANNIE: Come on, you bugger, be social. This boy. To get him
to talk to anyone!

(RICHARD *gets up and gravely shakes* LILLIAN's *hand, still
silent.*)

This is a friend of your father's. Come to ask if we know
where he is.

(RICHARD *just smiles.*)

LILLIAN: Do you?

(RICHARD *shakes his head slightly.*)

ANNIE: He likes to call at Christmas. Otherwise it's usually just
a cheque in the bank.

LILLIAN: Oh, really? And are they still happening?

ANNIE: Of course. He set up a trust when this one was born. So
it's fine.

(*She turns and walks back towards the cottage door.*)

EXT. FIELD. DAY

*The dog absolutely racing away from them at full speed into the
distance as* LILLIAN *and* ANNIE *walk through a high-summer field.
The sun is now even brighter, the Gloucestershire woods and fields
stretch away in front of them.*

ANNIE: It's not hard to talk. Why should it be? We had
different values that's all. We were both at school. So I was
his first proper girlfriend. We'd bunk off into town. Drink
frothy coffee and kiss under the pier. (*Smiles.*) Then later,
well, it became apparent . . . he couldn't just live. Just *live.*
Just be. Whereas all I wanted was living. He wanted
permanent romance.

LILLIAN: Yes.

(LILLIAN *smiles in recognition of this. She stoops for a stick to
carry as they walk on into the wood.*)

I've been going crazy. When he vanished, I thought it's
me. Even now, when he doesn't call. I wasn't sufficiently
romantic.

ANNIE: No. I don't think anyone is.

(*They stop a moment, listening to the day.*)

He came back one night twelve years ago. And nine
months later Richard was born.

(*They clear the wood. There in front of them is the river. It gleams in the summer sunshine, green and yellow, deserted.* ANNIE *sits down to undress, taking off her shoes.*)
Look, we'll bathe.
(LILLIAN *looks down at her undressing.*)
It's perfect. No one will see.

EXT. RIVER. DAY
From way above, the whole course of the river, seen snaking through the English countryside, a gleaming thread. Way down below, two heads bobbing together in the water.

EXT. RIVERSIDE. DAY
They have dressed and are lying side by side on the riverbank. Their hair is still wet, so their faces are fully revealed, both very white in the sunshine.
ANNIE: England's funny. You only get the point of it eight days a year. The sun comes out and you remember. You think, oh, yes, all this . . . (*gestures around her*) . . . all this around us – *that's* what it's for.

INT. COTTAGE. NIGHT
LILLIAN *is working beside the Aga. Beside her all the debris of preparation, vegetables strewn about, red wine.* ANNIE *is sitting at the table,* RICHARD *is leaning against the wall.* RICHARD *is quietly satirizing his mother.*
RICHARD: Look, she can cook.
LILLIAN: I haven't recently.
ANNIE: It smells wonderful.
(LILLIAN *reaches down and takes a perfect pie from the oven, which she sets down on the table in front of them.*)
LILLIAN: I tell you, I haven't done it for years. I've had no time. And yet I love cooking. (*Looks at them.*) I only remembered tonight.
(*They both smile at her.* ANNIE *looks down, moved.*)
ANNIE: That's great.

INT. COTTAGE KITCHEN. NIGHT
The remains of the meal in front of them. ANNIE *is sitting back in*

73

her chair, her legs against the side of the table, smoking a roll-up.
RICHARD *and* LILLIAN *are sitting contentedly listening.*
ANNIE: No. It never bothers me. I'm sorry for this one of
    course. (*Gestures at* RICHARD.) No fucking father, have

you? He has to put up with me all the time. (*Smiles.*) It's not what I'd recommend as a way of life. But if some perfect man came in tomorrow and said, 'Hey, let's fly away to Paris and fuck our brains out', I'd say no. I've got my garden.

LILLIAN: Huh.

(LILLIAN *frowns, thinking about herself.*)

RICHARD: That wouldn't take long.

ANNIE: What?

RICHARD: Fucking *your* brains out.

(LILLIAN *looks to see* ANNIE*'s reaction. It's hard to tell.*)

Anyway, personally I'd have said you were a bit past it.

(ANNIE *looks at him a moment, thoughtfully.*)

ANNIE: Isn't it time you went to bed?

INT. COTTAGE BEDROOM. NIGHT

Upstairs, in the cottage, two rooms are side by side. The guest room is spartan, a simple bed with low-beamed ceiling and plain white-washed walls. The two women are making the bed together, tucking the sheets in, putting a quilt on top. ANNIE *is talking as they work. We observe from outside in the corridor.*

ANNIE: Really, you know, *that's* my marriage, I mean with Richard, it's *like* being married, we know each other so well . . .

LILLIAN: Yes.

(ANNIE *picks up a spare pillow.*)

ANNIE: Even though in law I still have a husband . . .

(ANNIE *carries the pillow out of the room, towards us, and then passes from sight.* LILLIAN *has her back to us. She is now unpacking some clothes from an overnight bag. She has not yet heard this last remark. There are a few moments while she unpacks. We move steadily towards her back. And then suddenly we stop. She freezes, her back still to us. We are on the back of her neck.*)

INT. ANNIE'S BEDROOM. NIGHT

ANNIE*'s room is larger than the other, warmly lit with patterned bedspreads and a very large bed which dominates the room. The low lamps give it a slight art-and-craft feel, but there is a fair mess of untidiness, and a scatter of her interests – flowers, painting, reading*

75

– in sight. She is hanging up clothes, as LILLIAN *appears in the doorway with mock casualness. Her voice is gentle, quiet.*

LILLIAN: What? I'm sorry. What did you say?

ANNIE: (*Without turning.*) About what?

LILLIAN: You and Raymond. Did you ever get divorced?

(ANNIE *carries on with the clothes.*)

ANNIE: Saw no need to. Frankly it suits me fine. I never want to marry again. And Raymond, well, it gives him an excuse with the girls. He says, 'Oh, I'm sorry, I'd like to, but I just can't marry you.'

(*She looks up suddenly.*)

You know Raymond.

LILLIAN: Yes.

(LILLIAN *is still.* ANNIE *carries on making the bed.*)

ANNIE: And finally what sort of woman would want to marry him? I mean, people do acquire judgement. At least I have the excuse I was young.

(*She looks up.* LILLIAN *is smiling.*)

I'm sorry. Have I said something funny?

LILLIAN: No. It's silly. It's just . . . my excuse was that I was old.

(ANNIE *looks at her, not understanding.* LILLIAN, *embarrassed suddenly, helps her make the bed.*)

INT. MR CLARK'S ROOM. NIGHT

MR CLARK *is fast asleep in the bed. His face is pressed down into the pillow away from us. Through the venetian blinds, we see* LILLIAN *standing outside, a little breathless. The* STAFF NURSE *appears behind her.*

STAFF NURSE: He's asleep now.

LILLIAN: What happened?

STAFF NURSE: He was refusing medication. He says he won't take it. He made quite a scene. He's still quite powerful.

(LILLIAN *nods. Behind her in a little room across the corridor, a group of nurses are chattering among themselves, half watching the scene outside.*)

So I decided we'd best knock him out.

INT. MR CLARK'S ROOM. NIGHT

LILLIAN *approaches the bed. The* STAFF NURSE *stands some way behind.* LILLIAN *sits on the side of the bed. She puts her hand on his shoulder. He tenses, tighter into the bed, his face on the pillow.*

LILLIAN: Mr Clark? Mr Clark?

MR CLARK: Who is it?

LILLIAN: It's Dr Hempel.

MR CLARK: Go away.

LILLIAN: We need to talk.

MR CLARK: Fuck off.

(*She pauses a moment.*)

LILLIAN: I know you feel very strongly.

MR CLARK: I just want to die.

(*He sobs in the bed.* LILLIAN *looks to the* STAFF NURSE, *signalling her to leave. The* STAFF NURSE *goes.*)

I've been taking these things, I look in the mirror, I don't know who I am. It's not *me*. It's not *me*. It's this fucking *thing*. Just staring at me. It's not my face.

(LILLIAN *looks down. He still does not look up from the pillow.*)

LILLIAN: It's up to you.

(*She waits a second.*)

It's your right to refuse them.

MR CLARK: I'm going to die anyway. Aren't I?

LILLIAN: Well, I think that's right, isn't it? The drugs may help the pain a little.

MR CLARK: Fuck off.

(LILLIAN *waits a moment, then puts her hand on his shoulder.*)

LILLIAN: You don't have to take them.

(*He doesn't turn. But you can feel the acceptance of his victory. A moment's silence.*)

MR CLARK: I want to die as myself.

(LILLIAN *looks at him, thoughtful. Then Mozart begins to play.*)

INT. LILLIAN'S FLAT. DAY

A cry from AMY, *who is about to give birth.* LILLIAN'*s sitting room has been transformed into a progressive home-birth environment. It is dominated by an enormous wooden jacuzzi, which has been set up in the middle of the room.* AMY *is standing up, her feet in the water. Behind her, supporting her by putting his hands under her armpits, is* PHIL, *the midwife. He has a pink shirt which comes over his white trousers, which are rolled up around his feet. Opposite, in the water, is a* NURSE *who has also rolled up her blue jersey dress. A few friends of* AMY, *including* HUS, MADELEINE *and* IMOGEN *are standing nervously round the side. Mozart plays continuously.*

PHIL *checks across to the* NURSE, *making encouraging noises. Then a sudden climactic scream from* AMY, *and from* PHIL *an 'Ah yes'.*

INT. LILLIAN'S FLAT. DAY
LILLIAN *comes running at full belt into the flat, throwing down her bag, tearing off her coat as she comes. She runs into the sitting room, but just as she is about to go into the birth room,* PHIL *comes out through the partition door, blocking her way.*
PHIL: Please, please, some calmness.
(*He lifts his hands, smiling.*)
It is essential for the baby. Her first experience must be of peace.

INT. LILLIAN'S FLAT. DAY
On the other side of the doors, AMY *is now lying exhausted in the water. She looks up as* LILLIAN *comes in. Everyone lets out howls of pleasure.*
LILLIAN: Aaargh!
AMY: I know. Isn't it fantastic?
(*The* NURSE *hands the baby, naked, into* AMY's *arms.*)

INT. LILLIAN'S KITCHEN. DAY
Now excited activity at the sink, which is full of flowers being unwrapped and ice for all the bottles of champagne. The phone is ringing, the doorbell is going, a dozen people seem to have arrived, all chattering away. LILLIAN *is opening champagne and pouring into the glasses on* MADELEINE's *tray.*
MADELEINE: You must feel great.
LILLIAN: I'm so proud of her. Isn't it absurd?
MADELEINE: She'll be a good mother.
(LILLIAN *stops, the champagne suspended.*)
LILLIAN: Yes. I feel that.

INT. LILLIAN'S FLAT. DAY
The whole group now standing still round the jacuzzi, raising their glasses. AMY *now swathed in white sheets, still lying in the water.*
PHIL: To Mary. Years of happiness and health.
(*Silently they stand, suspended, glasses raised.*)

INT. LILLIAN'S BEDROOM. NIGHT
Darkness in the bedroom. The crib beside the bed. MARY *asleep. Beside her, in the bed, almost asleep,* AMY. LILLIAN *standing watching from across the room. Moonlight.* AMY *opens her eyes.*
AMY: What are you doing?
LILLIAN: I came for a look.
(AMY *smiles.* LILLIAN *looks into the cradle. Then sits on the side of the bed.*)
I've been very arrogant. I thought I was exempt. No one's exempt. You have certain feelings. And then you must pick up the bill.
(*She looks lovingly at her sister.*)
You've always known that. But it's taken me time.

79

(*She looks across at her, then goes over to the crib. Pinned to the wall are some pictures of dresses, spectacular, strapless.*)
When did you do these?

AMY: Oh, while I was waiting. I'd been fiddling, you know, all kinds of support. Straps and little bits of thing.
(LILLIAN *smiles at the drawing.*)
Then, you know, I decided, what would be easier? And what would look better?

LILLIAN: Nothing.

AMY: Exactly.
(LILLIAN *looks at her, then bends down and kisses the child.*)

LILLIAN: Goodnight, Mary.
(*She stands up, right by the window, moonlight on the side of her face.* AMY *smiles at her.*)

AMY: Let them stand up on their own.

INT. MR CLARK'S ROOM. DAY
MR CLARK'*s face. He has died.* LILLIAN *standing over the bed, very moved. She reaches for the sheet and covers his face. Opposite,* HELEN *is crying.* LILLIAN *looks down and, without saying anything, walks from the room.*

INT. HOSPITAL. DAY
LILLIAN *walks in a daze along the familiar corridor. She is resolute, calm. She seems unaware of everything around her. The trolleys, the wheelchairs, the usual rush. She comes out into the big lobby. From high above, we see her make her way, one figure in white among the crowds.*

INT. HOSPITAL CORRIDOR. DAY
We are on LILLIAN'*s back as she comes down another, distant corridor. At the far end, a door is open. A woman is sitting with her back to us on a laboratory stool, head bowed at work. She is silhouetted by the strong light from a big window in front of her. As* LILLIAN *reaches the room, she turns.*

LILLIAN: Romaine, I've changed my mind.

INT. HOSPITAL. DAY
Doctors, nurses, ancillary workers, cleaners all moving like a great surge towards the canteen, animatedly, laughing, full of good spirits.

INT. HOSPITAL CANTEEN. DAY
The doors of the canteen being kicked open by the advancing crowd.
Tables lifted. Chairs moved. The layout for a public meeting being
quickly improvised. A desk being slammed down at the front.

INT. HOSPITAL CORRIDOR. DAY
Now the corridors are deserted, except for a couple running in at the
last moment. In the far distance, LILLIAN *and* ROMAINE *are seen,*
heads bowed together, whispering, nervous. A sudden silence.

INT. HOSPITAL CANTEEN. DAY
There are a hundred people ranged round in a semi-circle. Chairs
everywhere, people sitting on tables, stretching away into the
distance. LILLIAN *slips in through a side door and walks alone to*
the table.
  ROMAINE *bangs her hand on the table for silence, and quietly*
LILLIAN *starts to speak.*

LILLIAN: I . . . this is not very easy. I've lived in England for
    quite a long time. I live my own life. I live it quietly. If
    anything, that is what's most attractive about this country.
    That no one will bother you. Unless you want. It's . . . I

can only say personally the reason I sailed here when I was twenty-five was for an idea of Englishness which perhaps was ridiculous, but which, incredibly, I have always managed to find. In my own country, for all its splendours, in the way we cure disease, there is an approach which seems to me not quite in line with the best interests of the people doctors are there supposedly to serve.

(*It is very quiet. She smiles, a little more confident now.*)

I'm told now to go on the offensive will only threaten this hospital. That if we are seen to be militant we will alienate the government, with exactly the opposite effect to what we would want. But if we do nothing – don't protest, don't organize – then we collude in the system's decline.

(*She smiles, anticipating her own point.*)

I sometimes reflect . . . a little bitterly . . . whether we who have come here, we the foreigners, don't care more about English values than the English themselves.

(SABOLA *laughs, in the front row. The rest of the multi-racial audience smile.*)

That's all I have to say. I'll be your chairman. For at least as long as I can. And I'll try to justify the confidence you've shown in me. Thanks.

(*She nods and sits down.*)

INT. HOSPITAL CORRIDOR. EVENING

The old team coming cheerfully down the corridor, full of energy and chatter. ROMAINE, SABOLA, HELEN, STAFF NURSE, GERRY *out of uniform.*

HELEN: That was wonderful.

LILLIAN: Well, it's a beginning.

ROMAINE: Do you think we fixed it?

LILLIAN: Sure. Now we just need the government to fall.

GERRY: Oh, well then . . .

SABOLA: No problems.

ROMAINE: There was one more thing actually . . .

LILLIAN: Yes.

ROMAINE: We wanted to ask.

LILLIAN: What's that?

(ROMAINE *looks to* GERRY, *who laughs.*)

ROMAINE: It was Gerry's idea.

LILLIAN: Go on, say it.

GERRY: Will you come and have a drink?

(LILLIAN *laughs*.)

LILLIAN: What is this?

ROMAINE: No, it's just . . . it's so long since we saw you.

(LILLIAN *smiles*.)

LILLIAN: Yes, I'd love to.

(*They stand a moment, all overwhelmed by the success of the moment.* Then LILLIAN *breaks.*)

Well, shall we go?

(*They all laugh.*)

INT. HOSPITAL LOBBY. NIGHT

LILLIAN, *perhaps after a few drinks, walks contentedly through the deserted lobby.*

INT. LILLIAN'S OFFICE. EVENING

LILLIAN'S *point of view as she comes down the deserted corridor towards her office. Her steps slow, anticipating, as if she knew there would be someone in there. Just before the door, she stops and looks through. A man is turned away from her like a cat burglar. He is in a suit. For a moment, you think it might be* RAYMOND. *He is putting an envelope on her mantelpiece, and now he turns, caught in mid-action, shamefaced. It's* IMRE.

LILLIAN: What is this?

IMRE: Oh, it's a present. I was asked to leave it for you.

(*She pauses a moment, as if dreading this. Then passes him to take the envelope down. Her name is on it and a hand-drawn rose in the corner. She looks at* IMRE.)

I got him a passport. I'm the one creditor he's managed to pay.

(*We are close on her hands over the desk, as she opens the envelope. It seems to be empty, but when she turns it upside down, out falls a tiny silver horse, identical to the one she has. She turns away, upset.* IMRE *watches her.*)

What's wrong?

LILLIAN: No, I'm happy. My faith's been repaid.

(IMRE *frowns, not understanding this remark. Suddenly he is terribly embarrassed. He rubs his hands on his suit pockets and begins to shift from foot to foot.*)

IMRE: Well, I must go. Julia is waiting. She has a very short fuse.

(*He fumbles towards the door.* LILLIAN *does not move, just letting him go. He turns at the door.*)

Are you all right? I can imagine what it's been like for you. If you need to send any message . . . or if there's anything you'd like to ask.

(LILLIAN *shakes her head.*)

LILLIAN: Nothing. It's fine as it is.

INT. BACKSTAGE. NIGHT

At once a strange quiet. We are in a huge dark space. At the far end of it calico has been hung on wires to make some improvised areas. Light bulbs shine from inside the areas. Otherwise it is dark. We move from a great distance towards the dressing area, catching little snatches of conversation and giggles as we approach.

LILLIAN: (*Out of shot*) How's it doing?

HUS: (*Out of shot*) It's good.

(*There is a peel of laughter from* LILLIAN.)

LILLIAN: (*Out of shot*) Oh, I can't believe it.

HUS: (*Out of shot*) It's right.

(*Now in front of us, other people are hurrying by. Strange costumes. A couple of girls in swimsuits, a man in evening dress, a gang of boys in T-shirts and shorts, a man in a Groucho mask and big white shorts.*)

MADELEINE: (*Out of shot*) How's yours? Mine's wonderful.

IMOGEN: (*Out of shot*) Mine's looking good.

(*We are getting very close now. A girl rushes by in a body stocking, clutching tulle in front of her. A couple of girls in pom-poms.* LILLIAN *calls to the next booth.*)

LILLIAN: (*Out of shot*) Amy?

AMY: (*Out of shot*) Yes.

LILLIAN: (*Out of shot*) Are you ready?

(*At exactly the same moment the curtains of the adjoining booths are drawn back. In each, there are three women, including* AMY, LILLIAN, MADELEINE *and* IMOGEN, *all in black strapless dresses, with* HUS *in attendance. The women come out to look at each other's dresses: they are all subtly different, but all shoulderless, cutting a line across the bust. The six women circle each other silently, the whiteness of their skin*

against the blackness of the dresses. They smile. AMY *is embarrassed. No one speaks. Then* AMY *raises her arms above her head.*)

AMY: They shouldn't stand up. But they do.

INT. HALL. EVENING

At once a burst of high-octane rock music. A huge church hall has been commandeered for an enormous party. Leading down from the stage is a catwalk which reaches out into the main part of the hall. There are two enormous banners reading FIGHT THE CUTS *and* FUND-RAISING BALL 1988. *There is very loud music as fifteen nurses walk down the catwalk wearing clothes they have made themselves – in a variety of styles. The audience is extremely enthusiastic, shouting, cheering, throwing streamers. There is a little row of photographers as at a proper show, lining the catwalk.*

INT. BACKSTAGE. EVENING

The women sit nervously in a row, waiting to go on, the blue curtain immediately behind them. Nobody speaks. The sound of the show in front of the curtain becomes increasingly distant as we move in from behind on the back of LILLIAN's *head, towards her ear. The sound of the fund-raising ball goes altogether and is replaced by the noise of a busy railway station.*

EXT. STATION. DAY

We cross-fade to a European railway station, very busy in the middle of the day. RAYMOND *is walking along beside a train, looking straight ahead. His clothes are different, shabbier, more relaxed than the suits we have seen him in during the rest of the story. He has his luggage on his back. He is oblivious to all around him. Then as he walks he suddenly notices a* GIRL *sitting alone on a bench reading a book.*

As he looks across to her, she drops her handkerchief accidentally on the ground.

He stops. He smiles. He moves towards the bench. He stoops. He picks up the handkerchief.

RAYMOND: You dropped this.

(The GIRL *looks up.)*

GIRL: Oh, yes. Thank you.

86

(She gives him a wonderful broad smile. He smiles back. And then suddenly he turns and begins to walk back in the direction from which he came.)

INT. BACKSTAGE. EVENING
The women rise to go on stage, all as one, up from their seats at the same moment.

EXT. STATION. DAY
RAYMOND *walks back along the platform, a wide, glorious grin on his face.*

INT. BACKSTAGE. EVENING
The women come to the curtain one by one and open it. Light blazes in their faces as they do. The cheers of the crowd. They all go through one by one, until LILLIAN, *last in line, reaches it.*
She stops a moment, about to part the curtain, as if she has just heard something behind her. She half turns towards us, listening.
And then she opens the curtain to go through.